Life in One Breath

Life in One Breath

Meditations on Science and Christology

Donald J. Lococo

Foreword by Sean J. McGrath

RESOURCE *Publications* · Eugene, Oregon

LIFE IN ONE BREATH
Meditations on Science and Christology

Resource Publications
An Imprint of Wipf and Stock Publishers
199 W. 8th Ave., Suite 3
Eugene, OR 97401

www.wipfandstock.com

PAPERBACK ISBN: 978-1-7252-9727-2
HARDCOVER ISBN: 978-1-7252-9728-9
EBOOK ISBN: 978-1-7252-9729-6

07/27/21

Edited by C. Claudia Galego
Front cover image by Donald J. Lococo
All photographs by Donald J. Lococo

For my parents, Rose and Anthony. *Requiescat in pace.*

God alone is the thought of the thinker and the content of the thought, the word of the speaker and the meaning spoken, the life of the living and the core of life itself.

—MAXIMUS THE CONFESSOR

Contents

Foreword by Sean J. McGrath | ix
Acknowledgements | xv

Introduction | 1
On Freedom | 13
On Creation | 37
On Beauty | 61
The Last Breath | 87

Bibliography | 95
Index | 99

Foreword

PERHAPS WHAT IS MOST striking about this slim but profound book—the fruit of a career researching and teaching science and religion—is the clarity of Don Lococo's commitment to both science and Christianity. Where many find a conflict here, and are compelled to compromise either the freedom of science or the sovereignty of revelation, Lococo sees complementarity—if not always harmony. In this regard, his approach more resembles that of the apostolic fathers than it does any of his contemporaries in the science and religion dialogue. Justin Martyr and Clement of Alexandria wrote over a millennium and a half before the methods of the quantitative natural sciences began to colonize the liberal arts. Theirs was a less flattened, and decidedly non-mechanized, understanding of nature. But they too were confronted by competing truth claims with regard to science and religion. Aristotle apparently required no transcendent principle to explain nature—the first mover is the pinnacle of nature, not a point of origin outside of it. Even where pagan philosophy suggested transcendence, as it did in Plato, the good beyond being (Republic VI), at least for pagan followers of Plato, was not a personal God, and so could not be the self-revealing subject of Judeo-Christian revelation. On the assumption that truth must in the end be one, the Fathers refused either to surrender revelation to natural reason, or to deny the legitimate insights of pagan philosophy. If Plato needed supplementation on this point from Paul, then Plato must be supplemented. And while the great Scholastic synthesis of theology and philosophy was still many centuries in the future, the Fathers did not regard the incompleteness of their explanations as an indication that either one or the other had to be sacrificed. Christianity and genuine human knowledge must be reconcilable, they assumed; if we fail to see how the two can be reconciled, the fault is ours. "For now we see through a glass, darkly; but then face to face" (1 Cor 13:12).

Lococo's approach to the very different challenges coming at Christianity from contemporary natural science shares the Patristic presupposition of the unity of truth, and of the inescapable limitations of our human capacity to grasp it. No doubt some readers will be surprised to find that Gregory of Nyssa and Maximus the Confessor are more vital to this book than Galileo and Darwin. But that is the kind of scholar Lococo is: a trained scientist whose heart he lost to theology. Science has everything to learn from this kind of two-sided thinking. Science, for Lococo, is never more reasonable than when it recognizes the limits of its methods, and never less so than when it presumes to be adequate to the full reality of the human and the divine. On the one hand, Lococo has no time for scientism and does not hesitate to point out where empirical methodology oversteps its boundaries (notably on the terrain of metaphysics, as it does with the question of beauty, as Lococo points out). But on the other hand, Lococo has no time for fideism, insisting that if the scientific community has reached a reasonable consensus on an issue that lies within its legitimate purview, then theology must recognize this and explain how such a view is compatible with Christian revelation. These two, scientific knowledge and revealed knowledge, are not on the same level, and this is what is most refreshingly Patristic about Lococo's book. The truth is one, but the means by which we come to know the truth are not, nor are they equal. The revelation of the divinity of Christ is no more accessible to empirical proof than are the principles of logic. But neither is revelation to be subjected to purely rational, metaphysical reasoning. In the revealed we know more and otherwise than we can naturally know.

It is this insistence on the unity of truth and the plurality of methods by which we achieve it which justified Lococo's attention to the otherwise heterogenous theological methods of Karl Rahner and Hans Urs von Balthasar, the two great Catholic systematic theologians of the twentieth century. Their inclusion as allies in the science–religion dialogue is another one of the refreshing surprises of this book. It is more common to pit these two giants of theology against one another, as the progressive and conservative representative of contemporary Catholicism respectively. Rahner ostensibly follows Protestant liberalism and prefers a Christology "from below," one that takes its cue from contemporary scientific and philosophical knowledge concerning human nature. Balthasar follows Barth (qualified in key places by Aquinas) and maintains a resolutely "high" Christology, demanding that the human and philosophical sciences rise to the occasion of recognizing in the crucified and risen Christ the revelatory form of God. But both Rahner and Balthasar, like Lococo himself, are deeply Catholic, and so equally united in their refusal of scientism, on the one side, and fideism, on the other. Ever since the First Vatican Council, the Catholic Church has defined the possibility (but not the adequacy) of a philosophical knowledge of infinite being. While the bishops who gathered at the First Vatican Council were a little more skeptical about the veracity of evolutionary science, the bishops who gathered at the Second Vatican Council were not. What the First Council declared about philosophy applies *mutatis mutandis* to the modern scientific knowledge of finite being (i.e., nature). Theology lets science be authoritative in its own proper domain.

What we discover in the course of Lococo's meditations is the generosity—the intrinsic plurality—of Catholic theology, and the immense resources it possesses for dialoguing with the sciences. Because Catholicism is not a system, it has room for both Rahner and Balthasar. And it refuses the false argument, generally coming from enthusiasts of science (distinct from scientists, most of whom know better) who have overstepped the limits of the scientific method, the commonplace falsehood that we must choose between a Christian view of humanity, its origins and possibilities, and a scientific view. Science may have demonstrated that some form of evolutionary natural selection took place, but it has not, and cannot, demonstrate that this evolutionary process was accidental or without intention or at the very least final causality. Even an atheist philosopher such as Thomas Nagel has begun to poke holes in the materialist account of evolution, arguing, tentatively, and not without some embarrassment over the awkwardness of the argument, in favor of natural teleology. If mind was not present in some form at the beginning of our natural history, Nagel argues in his 2012 *Mind and Cosmos*, then it cannot be present at the end. But mind is manifestly present; indeed, it is the condition of the possibility of your reading this sentence. That does not mean, of course, that mind must have caused the cosmos. But it does mean that it is reasonable to assume that mind was in some mysterious way present at the beginning. Nagel is not interested in arguments from intelligent design (and neither is Lococo, for that matter), and pursues his non-reductionist philosophy of mind in a purely atheistic and immanentist key. But his critique demonstrates what Lococo has long known: Darwinian evolution never disproved the existence of either mind or God. It only endeavored to explain how life developed on this planet, not why it began in the first place. Evolutionary science is only one place where thought inescapably finds itself asking metaphysical and theological questions; cosmology is another. But if a metaphysical question arises as a result of scientific investigation, Lococo argues, then it must be answered metaphysically. The same holds true for theology, with respect to both science and metaphysics. This is perhaps the leitmotif of Lococo's meditations on Christianity and science: Keep your instruments clean, and use them for the tasks for which they are best suited. It would not do to ask a geneticist to settle the question concerning human freedom, any more than it would do to ask an ethicist to settle a question in genetics.

This book is a carefully considered, long matured, and worthy follow up to Lococo's 2002 *Towards a Theology of Science*. We have perhaps not yet arrived at the theology of science, which Lococo argued in 2002 "does not yet exist." But with these meditations, Lococo has taken one more step in that direction.

Sean J. McGrath
Professor of Philosophy and Theology
at Memorial University of Newfoundland
St. John's, Newfoundland
January 26, 2021

Acknowledgements

I AM GRATEFUL TO my religious community for its love and support. The example of many scholars, most now with God, inspired me to make learning a daily experience. I acknowledge in particular the encouragement of Frs. Lawrence Shook, Armand Maurer, Harold Gardner, Terrance Forestell, and Michael Sheehan, who all supported my formative years as a scholar. As the only biologist in the local house, I was granted both more and less respect than perhaps I was due.

I thank also my colleagues in the Christianity and Culture Program at the University of Toronto: Mark McGowan, Janine Langan, Dan Donovan, and most especially, in memoriam, Joseph Boyle, the college principal, who hired and befriended me. And at St. John Fisher College, in memoriam, I acknowledge the support of Katherine Keough, who also hired me; Drs. Mel Wentland; and among the living, Tom Crombach, Greg Cunningham, Daryl Hurd, and the biology department; and Charles Natoli, Tim Madigan, and the philosophy department. The courses I taught in both departments served as propaedeutic to the work presented here.

I acknowledge the unfailing support of colleagues in the wider academy, particularly my friend and mentor Drs. Sean McGrath, in philosophy at Memorial University, Newfoundland; Erwin Huebner, my MSc supervisor at the University of Manitoba; and my PhD supervisor at the University of Toronto, the late Stephen Tobe. These three served most prominently as advisors throughout my career, instilling in me by example the work ethic I needed to do the best I can.

I thank Damian Hinojosa, of Saint Joseph Seminary College, Saint Benedict, Louisiana, my old and loyal friend of many years, who together with Sean McGrath and Michael Attridge—the latter at the Faculty of Theology, University of St. Michael's College, University of Toronto—reviewed the manuscript and provided valuable criticism and advice. I am humbled and grateful to them for their care and generous assistance.

I thank also my brothers, Jim and Richard, and all my myriad relatives who still treat me as if I was eight.

Finally, I thank Christina Galego, who throughout the process of composition, editing, and preparing the manuscript for publication, played an immeasurable role in the production of this work. Her graced instincts and gift with language and organization were essential to the final form of the work that follows. I am humbled by her dedication and buoyed by her encouragement. *Muito obrigado pelo presente que é você.*

Introduction

I COMPOSED THE ESSAYS collected in this book over the course of a life of Catholic faith marked by enthusiastic fascination with science. Although science had enthralled me since I was a child, it had not answered ultimate questions for me. Indeed, some questions I wanted to ask were well beyond its reach. If science characterizes only the physical and energetic dimensions of reality, I realized, there is little it can say of spirit or faith except what they are not. After completing my formal education by acquiring a PhD in biology, I taught university courses in faith and science at the undergraduate level, including in the Christianity and Culture program at the University of Toronto, and in the biology and philosophy departments at St. John Fisher College in New York.

Each of science and faith—apparently divergent realms of perception and inquiry—designates a unique approach to what *is*—to what has *being*. Considered in mutually respectful dialogue with one another, faith and science offer a broad view of reality that remains grounded in humility. But bringing them together, my teaching experience has shown, has been no small feat over the years, particularly in recent decades.

Before we turn to the essays, let us consider the conditions of the debate.

The Specter of Materialism

Materialism holds that all phenomena, including the activity of life, originate in the physical cosmos, which we encounter only through corporeal experience. Human culture has been haunted by its specter.

Arising from an atheistic interpretation of the scientific method's presupposition that only measurable things have truth value, it renders all other truth objects dubious at best. What have remained in its wake are the calculable contents of a universe consisting exclusively of matter and energy. On this account of human activity, matter looks for matter and finds it in abundance. Something is missing in the equation, however: that we look at all means that we have minds of lively aspiration that transcend the material.

In the age of materialism, the scientific method's prejudgment that God is not a scientific object has been taken to the extreme as the grounding presumption of all reality, that only matter is real whereas spirit is necessarily imaginary. In this move, having been rendered more than a method of empirical investigation, science as a form of human activity has become a negatively confessional meta-movement akin to a religion, complete with high priests, blind followers, and heretics, but minus any heart.

The ablation of the divine from the purview of science has meant that humanity alone is admitted to be history's steersman, charting an autonomous course through the tempests of personal and common experience of the chaotic forces of nature and culture. God simply does not enter the picture. Compared to the general public, 95 percent of whom believe in God, only half of today's scientists believe that reality is overseen by a power higher than that of humanity.[1] God as the source of all that is not divine, sustainer of every existent being, is irrelevant to science, which focuses singly on the sensible qualities of being, not on their ultimate

1. Liu, "Scientists and Belief," para. 2.
See also Rice University, ". . . [N]ot all scientists are atheists," para. 4–6.
This survey of U.S. scientists is largely corroborated by surveys in other countries.

origin or fundamental essence. Keeping its eye blind to ineffable origin, science is seemingly unimpeachable.

Scientism persists today lurking in the shadows of the academy, dividing scholars down confessional lines. Human life has always been taken with the abiding question: Why does the world exist? Traditional scholarship, which includes theology, philosophy, and the modern sciences, has sought factiously to answer this question, often hobbled by a lack of concerted focus on the ultimate cause that makes both subjects and objects of inquiry possible in the first place. Inquiry has become two-pronged, involving those willing to buy into an exclusively scientific worldview on the one hand, and on the other, those unwilling to ignore the long tradition of scholarship established, ironically, by communities of Christian faith in the first place.

Over the last quarter-century and more, the relationship between science and faith has been addressed by numerous scholars, resulting in the publication of a surfeit of books, many with titles so similar that it is difficult to distinguish between them. Many of these studies follow a course of specialized thought that has notably resulted in the near overpassing of the Catholic tradition of scholarship on the topic. Particularly conspicuous is the evasion of two of Catholicism's most significant twentieth-century theologians, who were dedicated to recovering the theological traditions of the early church to deal with what they viewed as materialism's threat to Catholic scholarship. Perhaps unsurprisingly, given such a sidestep, contemporary scholarship on the faith–science dialectic has been dominated by the kind of thinking both of these theologians eschewed.

The problem of human freedom in relation to God has opened the science and faith dialogue to the influence of Process thought, which posits that God, after creating a radically undetermined evolving universe, no longer interferes in its freedom. In this theory, freedom is preserved but God is subordinated from his position of infinity. Once granting us being, the theory contends, God respected human freedom by allowing it to be expressed without compulsion. It further contends that, as a result of this freedom, the progress of human activity affects and changes God. Along these lines, God's immanence in the world is thought to be contingent upon human freedom and, much as we are, capable of learning from that freedom's corporeal expression. That God is immanent is in itself not a problem for Christian faith. It is in fact a primary dogma of Christianity that the Holy Spirit indwells the universe, enlivening and sustaining its existence through divine grace. However, the idea that God *changes* at the behest of human freedom is ontologically topsy-turvy. In effect, it makes God dependent on the willful machinations of the divine handiwork—like an artist at the mercy of his portfolio.

Maximus the Confessor, a pivotal theologian in the seventh-century debate over whether Jesus had both a human and a divine will, wrote of the necessity of God's foreknowledge: "I do not believe that any reverent person should suppose that the things that were previously contained in the endless might of God's foreknowledge as ideas, God learns in detail through their coming into existence . . . God must recognize things as the products of his will."[2] For Hans Urs von Balthasar, any other account "would introduce passivity into God and, by doing so, would commit an anthropomorphism."[3] The error of anthropomorphism is the greatest error possible among those who dare to write about the ineffable.

Process thought emerged as a disciplinary compromise from an atmosphere dominated by the success of the scientific method, namely the spirit-dismissive atmosphere of modern materialism. It sought the middle ground between ancient tradition and modern philosophy. Most importantly, Process thought is a metaphysics that revises itself according to recent science, especially probability theory, and the general assumption of an evolving universe.[4] Not only did modernism throw out the baby with the bathwater;

2. Maximus the Confessor, "The Ambigua," in Balthasar, *Cosmic Liturgy*, 119.

3. Maximus the Confessor, "The Ambigua," in Balthasar, *Cosmic Liturgy*, 119.

4. This sentence reached its final form in consultation with Sean McGrath.

Process thought recovered the corpse, preserved its appearance, and stuffed it with the fruits of human frailty.

In view of this trend, the scientific method has disposed scientists to the illusion that they work for and toward the highest truth value in the academy. Although scientific materialism reached its peak as a system a century ago, its vestiges still linger. It has led to further internal division in an already divided Christian scholarship. In my view, there are two especially large lacunae in the current faith–science dialogue, owing to the near ablation from consideration of two of the most significant twentieth-century Catholic theologians, namely Balthasar and Karl Rahner. One can hardly conceive of building on the theology of any denomination without paying attention to its most deeply influential thinkers. The virtual exclusion of Balthasar and Rahner from such a vital conversation in favor of the culture they spent fifty years critiquing is the error I have sought to address in this book.

Each of the essays in this volume focuses on a traditional theme of theology of particular interest to the scholarly debate around faith and science: freedom, creation, and beauty. Rather than approach these topics with an exhaustive summary of the contemporary conversation—by including a literature review, for example—or conclude with a summary list of definitive theses, I have delved into the words of Balthasar and Rahner directly. Since the thinking and writing that occasioned these expository meditations emerges from a collection of lectures spanning several courses I developed across two decades of university teaching, the style of these essays is distinctly oratorical at times. As a priest who has given sermons and lectures in my time, my goal in these essays is to convey not only the substance but the spirit of our great theologians' teachings. The hope of these essays is that readers who have not yet encountered Balthasar and Rahner will not only be inspired to read them more closely, but to imagine anew their significance to the ongoing reconciliation of the work of science with the Catholic faith. The theological ground explored in these essays is meant to appeal memorably to readers, and in such a way that some part of their understanding is moved deeply.

If the faith–science debate has taught us anything, it is that the light of reason is as indispensable as it is finally inadequate to understanding. The following meditations on freedom, creation, and beauty will have served their purpose not only in illuminating the philosophical and doctrinal basis of this wisdom, but by enacting it in their very being.

The Life and Thought of Balthasar and Rahner

Readers already familiar with the life and writing of Hans Urs von Balthasar and Karl Rahner may wish to proceed directly to the essays—beginning with whichever topic inspires greatest interest. Readers who are approaching the theologians for the first time, or who would appreciate a refresher, are invited to keep reading.

Hans Urs von Balthasar (1905–1988) was a Swiss theologian who published over a hundred books and numerous articles over a long and prestigious career. He authored more books than most literate people read in their lifetime, which serves to illustrate at once the quality of his intellect and the magnitude of the error of his exclusion from contemporary faith–science discussions. Henri de Lubac, a French contemporary, said of his friend that Balthasar was the most cultured man in Europe. As a musician, he was remarkable: had he not entered the Society of Jesus, he could easily have become a concert pianist.

Balthasar's theology is grounded in the inescapable reality of the human condition in relation to God. Late in life, he wrote of "man" that he "exists as a limited being in a limited world, but his reason is open to the unlimited, to all of being. The proof consists in the recognition of his finitude, of his contingence: I am, but I could not-be."[5] One foundation of his theology can be stated simply as "the finite is not the infinite"—a resolution humanity has struggled with from the beginning.[6] Here Balthasar is deeply influenced by the Fathers of the Church, particularly Origen, Pseudo-Dionysus,

5. Balthasar, "A Résumé of My Thought," 469.

6. Indeed, Genesis 3 depicts humanity's first encounter with God as a power struggle marked by aspiration to equality with the maker.

and Maximus the Confessor. That we are limited in our ability to know and act is self-evident to every human being who has ever lived, regardless of the keenness of our intellect or the sublimity of our accomplishments. That we all were born, live a short life by cosmic standards, and die inevitably provides us with definitive proof of our finitude. Recalling Gregory of Nyssa, Balthasar affirms the illation that *we are not God.*

Influenced in Munich by Erich Przywara's focus on the analogy of being, Balthasar held that, as creatures whose being is the very image and likeness of God, human being is an analogy of God's infinite being. We possess the attributes of the divine image—delimited by our finitude. The supreme act of God's outreach is expressed in the divine freedom to create, which is the standard against which all created being is empowered in the act of its creation. Human freedom is real, even as it is constrained by the contingencies of life. It possesses the gift of a self-conscious capacity to choose to act or not act. And yet, Balthasar reminds us, for God to have left us to our own devices after gifting us with freedom would not have been in keeping with his infinite love and compassion, which are the reason anything other than God exists at all.

Drawing on Greek thought, the Church Fathers, and Mediaeval Scholasticism, Balthasar grounds his theology in the *transcendental attributes of being*: beauty, goodness, and truth—in which humanity participates finitely. In his trilogy on the transcendentals (consisting of fifteen volumes), Balthasar posits that the glory of God's infinite beauty so enraptures us that we wish to follow it not merely by choice, but out of a God-given quality of our being that opens us to its apperception. Our limitedness enables us to be free to choose the best possible relationship with infinite love. Beauty is thus not merely surface-sensed, but a fundamental attribute of all being, supremely revealed in God's glory through the death and resurrection of Jesus Christ.

Because our essence is modeled on the infinite truth that is the fundament of divine action, we rely on the God who has drawn us into glory as participants in divine goodness. The nature of divine truth is also relational, and *within* God's Trinitarian relation. In *The Glory of the Lord*, Balthasar writes:

> The relationship between Father and Son—that is the truth, and it goes without saying that one can get an insight into it only if one is oneself 'from God,' if one does not 'seek one's own honour' and 'abides' in the 'truth' which is the Word of God which both testifies and is testified to ([1 John] 8:13–58).[7]

God as creator has made truth be known by embodying it in creation, in his creatures—the consciousness of which, even of the highest so created, can only ever obtain but a small portion of reality rightly. Infinity has a way of making us humble—or so it should. Indeed, in our essence, we are possessed of the capacity and grace-given drive to continue to seek knowledge of all truth, ever moving toward that which we can only achieve if God actively draws us to it and reveals as much as we need to be ultimately united with God. Balthasar:

> From the standpoint of revelation, there is simply no real truth which does not have to be incarnated in an act or in some action, so that the incarnation of Christ is the criterion of all real truth (1 John 2:22; 4:2) and 'walking in the truth' is the way the believer possesses the truth (2 John 1–4; 3 John 3–4, etc.).[8]

For our meditation on freedom, we draw our inspiration from Balthasar's *Theo-Logic, Vol. 1* and *The Christian and Anxiety*, and for our meditation on beauty we draw upon his *The Glory of the Lord*.

Karl Rahner (1904–1984), another major contributor to Catholic thought in the previous century, was a contemporary of Balthasar. Although they were not always in agreement in their approach to theology, they were united in adherence to the precepts of revelation. They differed mainly in how they imagined theology could be applied to remind the modern world of the truths of revelation essential to enabling humanity to achieve its full potential

7. Balthasar, *The Glory of the Lord*, 135.

8. Balthasar, *Explorations in Theology*, 181–82.

in the world. Whereas Balthasar critiqued modernity for pushing aside the traditions preserved from the early church, Rahner attempted to make critical use of what was insightful in modernity's critiques—to incorporate the values wrought by and through modern science and the technologies that generate and are generated by its practice. Both men were apologists in the broadest sense[9] who defended the orthodoxy of Christian doctrine derived from revelation—both, significantly, through rational argument.

For his part, Rahner, SJ, was a Bavarian Catholic theologian whose theology covered nearly every important issue facing the faith. His theological purpose, the core of which was his study of Christ (Christology), has a unique historical role to play in the faith–science dialectic. Rahner was the first major Catholic systematic theologian to directly address the issue of the theory of evolution and its relationship to Christology. Even more difficult and controversial—and impressive—was his attempt to reconcile the biological model of human evolution in light of Christ's divinity and humanity. For Rahner, God, the "absolute ground" of human existence, created us in grace to be *receivers of the gift of grace* capable of going beyond the horizon of physical creatureliness and orienting our lives toward God. Rahner understood grace as the gift of Godself to humanity, *the revelation of being itself*, through which we share in all being.

For Rahner, human being is dependent on God's power, as grace, for both source and sustenance. Through God's universal saving will, we are preconditioned to be able to receive God's communication, in grace, in and through the humanity of his Son, who came to speak to us directly. We have access to divine grace also through the Holy Spirit, the abiding source of grace in the world, who maintains the cosmos in being, indwells the souls of the baptized, and continuously redeems them through resurrection grace. Rahner writes:

> [I]n grace, that is, in the self-communication of God's Holy Spirit, the event of immediacy to God as man's fulfillment is prepared for in such a way that we must say

9. For further reading, see Kilby, "Balthasar and Karl Rahner," 256–68.

> of man here and now that he participates in God's being; that he has been given the divine Spirit who fathoms the depths of God; that he is already God's son here and now, and what he already is must only become manifest.[10]

This capacity to be open to divine spirit is operative in us because we are human spirits in the world, material as all worldly beings are, but fundamentally spirit in the image of God, who is Father, Son, and Spirit.

Jesus Christ in his triune life is God become man, the meeting point between God and creation, incarnate in the world. Jesus's birth, life, and death show him as the real divine–human unity, the exemplar of all human life. Because God united divine nature to human nature in one divine person, we are assured in faith that we are embodied spirit. Thus, we are assured that God will raise *us* up to oneness with God in an analogous way.

In the process of addressing and integrating elements of evolutionary theory, Rahner reminds us that Jesus's humanity is the same as ours, except that his is without sin and in hypostatic union with divinity. The finitude of human nature as symbolized in our physical temporality is identical to Christ's. The processes of nature that determine human existence—be they material composition, growth through the various phases of human life and culture, or the requirements of physiology—all had an effect upon Christ's pre-resurrection life. The way that humanity as a species came to abide on earth pertains to all, including the Son of God. Any *mere* scientific study of the human race specifically, and of the life sciences more generally, is therefore woefully inadequate to the divine dignity and transcendent reality of the Lord in glory.

10. Rahner, *Foundations of Christian Faith*, 120.

On Freedom

THE HUMAN PERSON EMBODIES finite qualities that are substantive likenesses of the infinite, or in other words, phenomenal indications of divinity.[1] As "image of God" theology attests, in each power that is characteristically human, a facet of divine being glints from us uniquely. Human freedom is the most distinguishing of these aspects. Divine freedom is its paradigm—even though, in its infinity, divine freedom is completely other to human freedom's inescapable finitude. This analogy of being presents a paradox. Although the archetype is infinitely unlike creation,[2] God nonetheless charts the ultimate blueprint for each created being. God's infinite freedom thus provides the ground of expressible freedom in the created world. All finite beings, created freely by God, must, therefore, possess freedom to a finite degree. Herein emerges the initial question addressed in this essay: If humanity is in the image of God, in what sense and to what degree do all *animate* and *inanimate* beings also possess freedom? To answer this question, I will draw upon the first volume of Hans Urs von Balthasar's *Theo-logic: The Truth of the World.*

1. This chapter is a modification of Lococo, "Freedom and Intimacy in von Balthasar's *Theologic-I*," 114–35.

2. "In the contemplation of His essence, our comprehension and knowledge prove insufficient; in the examination of His works, how they necessarily result from His will, our knowledge proves to be ignorance, and in the endeavour to extol Him in words, all our efforts in speech are mere weakness and failure!" See Maimonides, *Guide for the Perplexed*, 83.

Disclosure of Hiddenness

Balthasar's philosophy of nature states that all levels of physical existence, both animate and inanimate, possess a freedom appropriate to their level of being. Humans may perhaps be able to identify freedom in their personal experience of life, but in what sense can *inanimate* objects or even simple animate beings be free? How does their freedom compare with ours?

Balthasar understands freedom as a being's capacity for disclosure, its capacity to conceal and reveal itself. Like Heidegger,[3] he understands truth as *aletheia*, a moment of unveiling. In disclosure, beings show themselves; yet this disclosure is always incomplete, gesturing beyond the world of appearances to veiled mystery. In the revelation of being, there is an aspect of the infinite that is not apparent. According to Balthasar, this quality of hiddenness is a feature of all beings—pre-animate, animate, moving, and thinking—albeit to different degrees. "The intimate character of being . . . has its preliminary stages in unconscious nature. There is no being that does not enjoy an interiority, however liminal and rudimentary it may be."[4] By attributing interiority to all physical beings, Balthasar does not thereby consider them to be completely inaccessible to knowledge. On the contrary, he maintains that the internal essence of being *does* "really manifest itself through the appearing phenomena."[5] No one who has witnessed the unfolding of a plant's life, he insists, could say that "he has seen 'only' the appearance of life, not its essence."[6] He simply denies that such interiority can ever be exhausted. "The inside lies concealed within an almost impenetrable veil: no scientific research will ever be able to explain what the vital principle is in itself. We see the facts, and they seem like unalloyed miracles to us."[7]

3. Corazzon, "Selected Bibliography on Heidegger's . . . *Aletheia*," 1700–27.
4. Balthasar, *Theo-logic*, 84.
5. Balthasar, *Theo-logic*, 84.
6. Balthasar, *Theo-logic*, 87.
7. Balthasar, *Theo-logic*, 85.

In short, all beings are not only permanently concealed but also, and to the same degree, permanently divulged. All beings consist of these two aspects—one that is understood and one that is yet to be intuited by future understanding—generating an endless process of investigation. Balthasar finds it apparent

> that reality, not merely by reason of some accidental circumstance, but by reason of an intrinsic necessity, must always remain richer than any cognition of it and that the truth even of the lowest level of being contains a richness that so utterly eludes exhaustive investigation that it can continue to engage inquirers until the end of time yet never ends up as a heap of unmysterious, completely surveyable facts. Something of the coquetry of veiling found in living things seems to belong already to material things; whenever the knower believes that he has got them once and for all, they slip away, leaving behind them a cloak of appearance.[8]

In their interiority, objects of scientific investigation are "not merely a passive prey for knowledge. At work even in them are energies that display themselves externally and thus move from the inside to the outside,"[9] an endless process that forever eludes us.

From this perspective, when we ask about any being, including ourselves, we plumb the depths of being itself and ultimately ask about the mystery of God. The dialectic process involved in the disclosure of all creation is ultimately a movement from personal divine being to personal human beings. The image of God, reflected in all beings and reaching created fullness in the self-consciousness of human being, points at once to the quasi-infinity of the created and the true infinity of the uncreated. Balthasar summarizes his Christian philosophy of the interiority of being as an image of the hiddenness that God has revealed, one that yet remains eternally mysterious:

> Along with their own being, God has given to all created things their own operation, and this includes a

8. Balthasar, *Theo-logic*, 86.

9. Balthasar, *Theo-logic*, 86.

> spontaneity in manifesting themselves outwardly, an echo, however distant, of his infinite, majestic freedom. Every entity that has being-for-itself possesses an inside and an outside, an intimate and a public sphere. The intimate dimension of beings can appear in a great variety of forms and on a great variety of levels. It increases as things move up the scale of being-for-itself; it reaches its complete form on the level of self-conscious spirit. On this level, the exteriorization of the interior is left to the discretion of the spirit and is thereby protected from being grasped mechanically by any stranger's knowledge. Yet even sub-spiritual entities are not completely bereft of this kind of protection. Every level of being possesses a characteristic form of this protection that differs from that of the others, a special mantle received as a gift from the Creator. This protection gives each particular unveiling and revelation of a thing the character of a solemn act, occurring only once, in which the inexhaustible newness of truth overpoweringly manifests itself.[10]

In this way, he accounts for differences in the disclosure of diverse beings in terms of their receptivity to other beings. From single-celled organisms to nonhuman primates, he observes increasing subjectivity corresponding to a gradation of increasing self-consciousness and intelligence. He observes that entities without consciousness, such as stones, have no receptivity. By extension, he reasons, "their essence is closed to itself, and so they are unreceptive to everything around them; because they are not subjects, there are no objects for them."[11] In other words, there is a direct correlation between consciousness and receptivity to other beings, on one hand, and on the other, between a being's capacity for interiority and its capacity for disclosure. And it is in these terms that Balthasar accounts for varying degrees of interiority in various beings. Plants, for example, "are capable of assimilating some little part of their environment, but they do so without

10. Balthasar, *Theo-logic*, 82.

11. Balthasar, *Theo-logic*, 82.

becoming inwardly aware of the other as such."[12] In view of their lack of receptivity to others, he designates plants as "entities with less perfect interiority." In keeping with this assessment, so too have animals[13] limited interiority: "To be sure, their sensorium unlocks them to the outside world and grants them a certain perception of otherness. Nevertheless, because they lack self-consciousness, they are likewise incapable of setting the other over against themselves *as other*."[14]

Animals, both predators and their prey, have a keen sense of otherness, but only at the instinctual level, not at the intellectual level of mutually recognized self-consciousness. Self-conscious awareness of otherness is the privilege and the onus of human beings. Balthasar writes: "The world is unlocked in its objectivity only to man, because his self-consciousness gives him the measure of being."[15] Only humans are aware of self as the *inner other* and are thus able to recognize the *outer other* as a like being. Balthasar recognizes that the transition from the subthreshold consciousness peculiar to animals to human consciousness "radically changes the situation of epistemology: the object is now itself a subject." A stone has no consciousness and thus there exist no objects for it; with the emergence of full human consciousness, however, nonhuman others become disclosive objects for humanity. Even though we possess full self-consciousness, the human other can never be purely an object for us, insofar as each human is possessed of an interiority that is subjectivity.

12. Balthasar, *Theo-logic*, 45.

13. Notwithstanding the defensible scientific accuracy and moral thrust of the term "nonhuman animals"—as distinct from "human animals" (a designation underscoring humans' belonging to the animal kingdom)—Balthasar's traditional terms retain theological significance. See, for example, Balthasar, "On the Concept of the Person," 18–26.

14. Balthasar, *Theo-logic*, 45.

15. Balthasar, *Theo-logic*, 45.

Truth Disclosed

Positing the interiority of being with respect to the experience of otherness, Balthasar emphasizes the importance of the one to whom a being discloses itself. The beauty of a flower opens up in the consciousness of the human observer, giving the flower its fullest expression of disclosure while simultaneously reserving its hidden intimacy. In this dialectic, the observer must catch as much of it as he is able to grasp, because the disclosing source is infinite, even as the observer is finite. In other words, "The truth of any being will always be infinitely richer and greater than the knower is capable of grasping."[16] This truth was evident also to Heraclitus at the dawn of philosophy: "Things keep their secrets."[17] The impenetrability of objects operates also in intersubjective knowledge, wherein the subject may become bewildered "that the objects waiting to be known also have an inner sphere and are thus knowers in their own right."[18] From this perspective, Balthasar maintains that "we can no longer speak of *the* subject, as if there were just one, but only of a plurality of subjects, each of which possesses and knows its truth first of all for itself and whose intersubjectivity raises a host of new and difficult questions."[19]

In addressing the problem of defining intersubjectivity, we cannot think of living things as mere objects of understanding; we must think of them as living co-subjects capable of experience—even if they do not think of themselves as such. This is most obvious in the case of our observations of higher primates, who, if they are aware of human presence, are impossible to study without accounting for their consciousness of being observed by the researcher. Their behavior is *influenced* by their awareness of being observed by creatures recognizably similar to themselves. As such, the scientist does not so much observe the "wild" behavior

16. Balthasar, *Theo-logic*, 88.

17. Heraclitus, "Fragment 10," in Brooks, *The Collected Wisdom of Heraclitus*, 9.

18. Balthasar, *Theo-logic*, 89.

19. Balthasar, *Theo-logic*, 89.

of the ape as she studies how an undomesticated ape is affected by scientific observation. The ape, though possessed of nonhuman intellect, cannot be regarded as merely an object. According to Balthasar, we can only ever know very little—beyond obvious responses such as pain and pleasure and reproductive drive—about what an animal cognizes:

> What does an animal see, hear, and feel? We do not know now and we will never know in the future. The world of sensory images is purely subjective and, as such, cannot be objectified. To be sure, the scientist can, on the basis of comparative studies of sense organs in animals, draw certain analogical inferences about how animals perceive. That they do in fact perceive, indeed, that their perception is analogous to that of the subject performing these studies, is indisputable.[20]

Acknowledging that it would be unworthy of serious natural science to classify animals according to their reflex mechanisms, he nevertheless maintains that we can "never share animals' experience of how they actually see or of what they actually feel when they show outward signs of pain or joy."[21] In this way, animals are analogously "selves"—even if they are unaware of it. That said, if we someday find a common language with whales, the evident joy of a dolphin's leap will be forever hidden from us.[22] Nor will they ever understand our delight in observing them.

Although all beings necessarily possess interiority and hiddenness in their limited showing of self, Balthasar contends that none but humans are *self-conscious*, supremely so in the God-man Jesus Christ. While intimacy grants all beings subjectivity peculiar to their level of self-awareness and receptivity, Balthasar maintains

20. Balthasar, *Theo-logic*, 89.

21. Balthasar, *Theo-logic*, 90.

22. According to the tenets of information theory, there is little doubt that whales communicate via language. Bottlenose dolphins have been shown to possess and elocute a repertoire of twenty-seven single-letter syllables, five two-letter syllables, and four or five three-letter syllables. What meaning they may translate has yet to be determined. See Smith, "Complexity in Animal Communication," 1–17.

that only self-conscious being can be conscious of *solitude*—that is, can be personally aware of interiority. Solitude is inescapable even in a crowd; it is both the gift and sorrow of free beings. The self-conscious being possessed of subjective interiority

> must content himself with having a worldview and answering for it in his own name with a responsibility that he can never shove onto another. For he does not know how the other sees the world. Even if the other saw it in the same way, one could never be finally certain that the other's world picture was in fact the same. Moreover, the knower must acknowledge these limits imposed by the other's self-being by letting go of the other's self.[23]

The uniqueness of individual subjectivity determines that, for each subject, there is a unique worldview delineated by the authenticity and wisdom of a singular self-consciousness. While this provides the basis of solitude, it also establishes the basis of intersubjective love: letting the other be—both shown and hidden. Without this distance, Balthasar maintains, "there can be no proximity of minds; without this reverence before the other's self-being there can be no love."[24] And it is this love that is the basis of our responsibility as stewards over the animal kingdom. It is our responsibility to let sub-rational beings be what they must be, what they ineluctably "tell" us they are (*aletheia*).

No animal can possess a human worldview, but even animals have unique worldviews peculiar to the genetic limits of their species, albeit minus the full self-awareness of a human worldview.

> The animal kingdom gives rise to a variegated profusion of subjective images of the world, all of which are closed off from one another. Each of these images is completely finite; it operates within a peculiar environment that is snugly fitted to its particular sensory apparatus . . . [W]e cannot imagine what a sensorium without a mind would be. These images of the world live alongside us and partially overlap our own. Alien worlds that we will never

23. Balthasar, *Theo-logic*, 90.

24. Balthasar, *Theo-logic*, 90.

> know pass right through ours, and sentient beings are separated by distances for which there is almost no common measure.[25]

That we act as stewards is not a limitation determining our separateness from them, but an indication of our congruity with them. What we say about their being, which brings their self-showing to a fullness that is otherwise *always* hidden, gives language to the silent words that their being names for us.

> Nevertheless, sentient creatures[26] are rooted in a medium of life common to all. All of them have an outward form that, in its own way, is as significant as a clearly articulated word. Nature has produced an immense number of such words—as many as there are genera and species of living things. And whereas plants are only spoken words, animals speak as much as they are spoken. Animals, unlike plants, are not merely a voice that takes form from within: they have a concomitant sensibility by which they are aware of this process of formation. They do not merely express something; they express themselves.[27]

Human self-consciousness parses the grammar of the human word, and in our studies, translates nonhuman self-expression into intelligible human language. Only through our translation-mediation does the intimate character of sub-self-conscious being reach its fullest expression. Relatively unfree as nonhumans are to disclose what lies within them, human freedom enables an ever-greater explication of their disclosed truth. In the process,

> [t]hey themselves have a share in the movement from inside to outside, in the exterior communication of themselves, in their truth. They stand midway between freedom and unfreedom. They have the freedom to express themselves outwardly in some form of audible or

25. Balthasar, *Theo-logic*, 91.

26. Sentient in this case means having a capacity to sense their environment. A misleading modern meaning is having a rational capacity. The latter is not the biological meaning of this term.

27. Balthasar, *Theo-logic*, 91–92.

> inaudible language. But they do not yet have the freedom to express themselves when and how they wish.[28]

We assist them by speaking for them.

Clearly, the full character of human freedom is grounded in a necessary interrelation with sub-rational being. Human freedom emerges from unfreedom, much as we are genetically ancestrally linked to animals. We can interpret what sub-rational beings show of what they *are*, but we are unable to know fully *what* they are or *how* they show it. For, "everything about the animal eludes us, not because it is inaccessible to awareness, but because it is the animal, and not we ourselves, who becomes aware of it."[29] Although the animal's awareness is non-conceptual and their interiority remains hidden, what they show is "not just objective expressions of life but subjective ones as well."[30]

In their inability to self-express firsthand without our help, animals remain more mysterious to us than we are to ourselves. This interdependence of dialogue makes understanding possible. The reliance of medical research on animal intimacy to increase understanding of our physiological "intimacy" illustrates this fact clearly. Their limited freedom enables our objective understanding of subjectivity.

> The movement in which they express themselves happens necessarily and is bound to a predetermined natural language. We do not understand this language immediately. We believe we can, at least in part, interpret its meaning . . . What we do know for certain is that even what is obscure to us is the expression of life, which speaks meaningfully in its own words insofar as its exterior communication corresponds to its interiority. Every word in the vast language of nature speaks itself, without knowing the sense of the others.[31]

28. Balthasar, *Theo-logic*, 92.
29. Balthasar, *Theo-logic*, 92.
30. Balthasar, *Theo-logic*, 92.
31. Balthasar, *Theo-logic*, 92.

Each being speaks a word no other being, except God, can fully glean. It is a measure of the uniqueness of being. We attempt to draw all "meanings" together and interpret their interdependent unity to the best of our cognitive powers. For, without us, the manifold voices of created being remain God's Word, naturally spoken, echoing eternally, waiting to be heard, interpreted, and understood. We can make coherent sense out of the apparently random facts that show the living principle that informs our life.

> Yet the immensely coherent discourse that results is proof that this language emerges from a common fund of life that finds endless ways in which to express itself. The testimony of life reaches beyond the solitude of the individual word, which bears witness to a separate interiority. Life attests that it is a totality by the coordination of so many voices and fields of expression.[32]

Freely we gather our individual human words together with the words spoken by each being that "life attests," motivated by our hunger to know how multiplicity is grounded in apparent unity. The ever-expanding sensorial assistance, both natural and technological, continuously informs the community of scholars about the data we interpret to revise our understanding of the truth of beings.

Human Freedom

Human self-consciousness reflects an inner dimension that Balthasar calls "light for itself." Self-possession makes us self-consciously free. We are "substantially spirit" and therefore unique. Balthasar writes: "To the extent that man is spirit, he can dispose of himself. Hence, he can decide whether and how he shall make his utterances. Freedom enters between the spirit's self-possession and its self-expression, between the interior and the exterior word; it becomes an integral component of the truth."[33]

32. Balthasar, *Theo-logic*, 92.

33. Balthasar, *Theo-logic*, 93.

In human life, when the inner dimension of being opens us up to self-disclosure, subjectivity reaches full self-consciousness. Freedom determines not only our ability to express interiority externally, but also the authenticity of its expression. Truth expressed becomes inseparable from truthfulness of the expresser. "Man freely disposes of truth, for it has been placed in his hands and committed to him to administer self-consciously. He is the first entity that can freely tell the truth, but for the same reason he is also the first that is capable of lying."[34]

The freedom to deceive has given humanity an edge in evolution, enabling survival over sub-rational predators possessed only of instinctual guile.[35] Deception, to some degree common among animals, is relational. Sometimes we deliberately attempt to alter the flow of disclosure from the interior to the exterior, with questionable results. Self-deception is self-defeating in the deliberate distortion of self-consciousness.[36] The transcendental character of being-true, moving from interiority to exteriority, unveils the character of the good. Self-conscious being can freely choose to embrace the goodness of truth. Non-self-conscious being is necessarily good.

A flower in bloom is incapable of denying that it is ready for insects to pollinate it. The truth disclosed to animals is necessarily revealed, and interpreted instinctively. A male silkworm moth cannot help but follow the concentration gradient of pheromones the female releases upwind miles away. This is not necessarily the case for humans. Balthasar explains: "In man, this objective truth is accompanied by subjective truth, which is the capacity to possess for oneself the measure between the thing and its expression.

34. Balthasar, *Theo-logic*, 93.

35. Deception is a crucial behavioral device in primate evolution. Fooling your predator betokens intelligence sufficient for personal survival and, collectively, that of the species. See Rue, *By the Grace of Guile*.

36. "Deception occurs when a discrepancy between appearance and reality can be attributed in part to the causal influence of another organism. That is, a deceiver is an organism (A) whose agency contributes by design to the ignorance or delusion of another organism (B). Self-deception may be said to occur when A and B are the same organism." Rue, *By the Grace of Guile*, 88.

The object of knowledge becomes the subject of knowledge. Being coincides with consciousness in self-consciousness, thus becoming its own object. This is the true meaning of the *cogito ergo sum*."[37] Self-conscious knowing and acting are the distinguishing characteristics of the spirit-being. "The spirit receives two gifts simultaneously: the gift of knowing the truth and the gift of saying it. It would be unthinkable if it obtained only the first gift without the second."[38] The freedom to self-reveal is the freedom to give as much as one wishes the other to know.

Beyond the necessity for cognition in self-conscious being (we cannot *not* think), Balthasar's salient point is that our freedom to disclose also empowers us to discretion.

> Being's revelation to itself also immediately enables and thus requires its revelation to others. But from henceforth this revelation is free. Even though man is predisposed to communication in general, he is not compelled by nature to any one conscious communication in particular. He does not have to say what he knows. He has the command of his treasury of knowledge, so that he can make a free gift of every particular disclosure. No one can wring his truth from him or manipulate it without his knowledge and consent . . . Precisely when truth comes wholly to itself, when a being's unveiling is possessed and understood as such, truth is no longer something accessible to everyone in general but is a free, personal reality.[39]

Not everyone can be trusted with the deeply intimate nature of personal subjective truth. Friends can benefit from our truth, as we can too in our revelation of it to them—hearing it anew as they hear it—but even they can abuse it. Enemies can distort our truth or use it out of context to diminish our freedom to disclose other truths. The truth's premature utterance can mislead the other's thinking, especially if they are not privy to the method used to decipher it, or if they do not possess a comparable breadth of

37. Balthasar, *Theo-logic*, 93.

38. Balthasar, *Theo-logic*, 93–94.

39. Balthasar, *Theo-logic*, 94.

intuitional experience, or if they are unskilled in the cogitative process. As a gift given to another, disclosed truth is subject to the good intentions of both giver and receiver.

> The communicator has the freedom to dispose of his truth as he wishes . . . This decision is an ethical act, whose justification is subject to the laws of ethics. The actual communication consists in the fact that the communicator gives outward expression to the truth that he possesses in his intimate sphere . . . It must have the curious ability to grant a glimpse into itself, without for all that laying bare its soul to the other's casual inspection.[40]

Balthasar's point is biblical: "Do not give dogs what is holy; and do not throw your pearls before swine, lest they trample them under foot and turn to attack you" (Matt 7:6).

While our capacity to be agents of what we disclose distinguishes us from animals, the human spirit is also circumscribed by the body's evolutionary past. Free disclosure depends upon the human organism, which is enslaved to the necessities of nutrition, concupiscence, personal emotions, and psyche, all of which reflect and determine personal histories within the biosphere of living natural history. As Balthasar says, in our disclosure of personal truth, "the specific features of spiritual intimacy are inextricably inter-woven with all the forms of sub-spiritual interiority, above all with the intimacy of the sensorium."[41] Self-knowledge is not merely thinking-awareness of being. All self-understanding derives from intuition of sense data gathered by our flawed and easily fooled sense organs, the windows to human consciousness. The infinity of human interiority cannot be reflected fully in a self-possessed being-for-itself, because we perceive ourselves via the same flawed sensorium, linked necessarily to motor neurons that control our movement. Balthasar writes:

> [It is] not just that man's spirit can be present and unveiled to itself only when it comes to itself from the

40. Balthasar, *Theo-logic*, 94–95.

41. Balthasar, *Theo-logic*, 97.

> self-estrangement entailed in knowing objects. There is rather the further reason that man's very self-possession is never a perfect knowledge of his essence. The spirit is unveiled to itself only to the extent that it knows its existence and certain fundamental characteristics of its quiddity, but its gaze does not penetrate to its inmost essence. The full depth of its origin, structure, possibilities, and freedom remains concealed from it.[42]

In other words, our blindness to the full depth of personal being is a measure of the limit of our freedom. We necessarily search for what is forever elusive. This is the ineluctability of spirit that enables our freedom but commits us to an endless search for absolute knowledge and freedom. Only in God can we find both.

For Balthasar, intimacy *is* freedom, a quality of being that is known to us both in the privacy that we withhold from disclosure and the personal mystery we seek to disclose to ourselves. In the nakedness of free intimacy, all beings are one in freedom with the infinite source. We seek to unfold personal intimacy, and in our subjective frustration, project our inquiry onto the intimacy of other beings, endeavoring to understand objectively what is hidden in their intimacy. The mystery within and the mystery without are both subject to incrementally induced disclosure through human inquiry. But they may also be driven into further concealment. From a theological perspective, science violates the freedom of the object by plundering its interiority; science can never exhaust an object's infinite movement from essence to existence. Knowledge can be pursued otherwise. By amplifying the object's disclosure in scientific study, by bringing to visibility what otherwise remains invisible, knowledge realizes the object's freedom to act. Inquiry can thereby increase rather than restrict freedom. This is the task of a theology of nature.

As we have seen, within the intimacy of a self-reflective spirit resides the freedom inherent to living being that is proportional to its capacity for self-consciousness. Human freedom differs from that of our nonhuman fellows in that, in our meta-cognition of it,

42. Balthasar, *Theo-logic*, 97.

our freedom can be erroneously employed to choose *nothing* over being. The Fathers thought of non-being as equivalent to sin. The paradox here is that the "choice" of sin over goodness is the choice of not choosing. It is an act of hubris given its pretentiousness in the face of One who knows all. We act creatively like God, but engender a sham—an act of unfreedom. So it is indeed appropriate to speak of a life marked by wrong choices as "a tale told by an idiot, full of sound and fury, signifying nothing."[43] In sin, we choose to no longer abide in divine freedom, instead choosing nothing at all. In so doing, suffering enters our lives, not through choice, but through its lack.

Freedom's Limits: Original Sin and the Origin of Suffering

In all major religious traditions, suffering is a fundamental existential quality of living being. In Christianity, suffering is Christic atonement for sin. Building on the Genesis account of the Garden, the New Testament reveals that the earliest Christian communities believed human nature to be fallen. Figuratively inheriting the original sin of Adam, humanity persists today in an estranged state from God, enduring punishment for the common and primordial desire to be like God. In each generation, humanity consistently refuses to embrace its creaturely difference from the creator and aspires to be divine. Like children pretending to be adult to compensate for childish finitude, we in sin aspire to *be* God to compensate for our finite humanity. Sin is a futile attempt at reverse creation. As the Genesis narrative relates, playing God is the root of all other sin.

Humanity shares a common delusion that, by will, it can graft divinity onto human nature, and become God-like. The original innocent relationship with God, marked by faithful certainty of God's solicitude, is now denied to all Adam's descendants. If this primordial "Fall" is indeed the original human sin, which has God-blinded us from our original intimacy, then the anxiety that

43. Shakespeare, *Macbeth*, act 5, scene 5, lines 25–27.

haunts us is divine absence and not a quality of our original created being. Balthasar writes:

> . . . God did not create anxiety as a component of nature, and all of the distance or remoteness within nature . . . would be partially determined, in its concrete reality, by the distance of the sinner from God, by the falling dynamic of guilt. Partially determined, and not simply determined, because from another perspective the ontological difference is by necessity the very expression of creatureliness itself, in whatever state the creature may be. But partially determined in such a way that the modality of transcendence and contingency as we have sketched them could not be explained otherwise than through a falling away.[44]

Distance from God, *as* finite being, is the grounding necessity of creatureliness, the distinguishing reality that separates our individual being from the source of being. In addition, however, there exists emptiness, perceived within our hearts, that is caused by our active turning away in sin from the source of life. This void of emptiness is the result of us seeking in finitude the consolation Adam once enjoyed in the divine presence. The ontological difference between human and divine nature is thus the matrix upon which God's further withdrawal from human certainty becomes punishment for sin. What was once an open door of sureness was slammed in our faces. Balthasar contends that God's withdrawal is the root cause of human angst.

The scriptural source of the Fall[45] in Christian tradition is found in Ps 51:5 and Paul's writings (Rom 5:12–21, 1 Cor 15:22), which texts comprise the theological sources of Original Sin later

44. Balthasar, *The Christian and Anxiety*, 133.

45. A fall might be an accident or caused by another agent. "The Fall" might more rightly be called "the Jump," because we do the latter willfully.

developed by Irenaeus[46] and Augustine.[47] The dogma of Original Sin states that humans, born in a state of sin, are predisposed to willful sinfulness later in life. The foundational source of this dogma is the creation account of Genesis 2.[48] In this mythological account, Adam and Eve live contently in the Garden while reveling in the consolation of God's special favor to them. Their faith relationship with God is the natural reality of human existence, a reality intended by God to be the norm for human life.

God created the human person in the image and likeness of absolute love, the consummate expression of divine freedom. God created us in the image of freedom, but not in freedom's infinite fullness. Human freedom *is dependent upon* and *necessarily limited by* divine freedom, its archetype.

> The more completely man participates in God's freedom, the freer he is, and it is only within the realm of God's freedom that man can realize his potentiality for freedom. It becomes clear at the same time that man cannot stand

46. "And thus, as the human race fell into bondage to death by means of a virgin, so is it rescued by a virgin; virginal disobedience having been balanced in the opposite scale by virginal obedience. For in the same way the sin of the first created man (*protoplasti*) receives amendment by the correction of the First-begotten, and the coming of the serpent is conquered by the harmlessness of the dove, those bonds being unloosed by which we had been fast bound to death." Irenaeus, "Against Heresies," in Roberts, Donaldson, and Coxe, eds., *Ante-Nicene Fathers*, vol. 1, 547.

47. Regarding his mother, Monica, Augustine writes: "[T]he torments which she suffered were proof that she had inherited the legacy of Eve." Augustine, *Confessions*, 101.

48. It is a matter of debate whether Original Sin is a doctrine in Judaism. First posited by Irenaeus and later elaborated by Augustine, Original Sin was based on the Hebrew word for sin, "*cheit*," in the Gen 3:17–19 expulsion narrative, versus "*yester ha-ra*," used by Paul. Like Paul (Rom 5:12), some Talmudic scholars hold that Adam's sin was inherited. For example, Maimonides thought that Adam's sin made him lose the capacity for pure rationality (see Maimonides, *Guide for the Perplexed*, 12–13). However, most Jewish scholars contend that humans sin because they are not perfect beings (*cheit*), not because humans are inherently sinful (*yester ha-ra*). See the Jewish Virtual Library, "Issues in Jewish Ethics: Judaism's Rejection of Original Sin."

> vis-à-vis God as his "partner," for "he is the all" (Sir 43:27) and cannot therefore actually have an opposite number.[49]

Consequently, from the time of Adam's creation, the contingent limitations of creaturehood marked his relationship with God—the finite with the infinite, the creature with the creator. Adam's descendants are more than a mirror image of God—transitory but still substantial—and infinitely less than being God's equal—a condition to which Adam and Eve had sinfully aspired. All the divine attributes that humans possess are *necessarily* limited by their being derived from their absolute source. God had not recreated divinity in Adam and Eve, generating divine copies of God's self in them. Yet Scripture reveals that the first humans aspired to such greatness for themselves. The mythological account of paradise is thus God's revelation of the limitedness of being human.

Adam and Eve could not know what "knowledge of evil" meant before their fall from grace, because they were always in the presence of God and had no experience of not-God. They chose instead forbidden knowledge gained from the fruit of the tree of paradise, thus falling from the special grace of God's intimate faith-presence. Their disobedience led them not to knowledge or God-like powers, but to the unforeseeable opposite: the capacity of knowing non-being.

> We are not saying that Adam saw God face to face, for if that had been true, his subsequent falling away from God would be inexplicable. We are only saying that the space within Adam that became a place of emptiness and indifferent freedom through the withdrawal of the divine presence was a space that God had originally created for himself and had filled with his mysterious and, on the other hand, unquestionable presence. It was a presence in faith, naturally, but it occurred in a now no longer attainable obedience and love that possessed and embraced God immediately and with childlike certainty.[50]

49. Balthasar, *The Moment of Christian Witness*, 82.

50. Balthasar, *The Christian and Anxiety*, 135.

Once marked by the experience of an alternative choice *other* than the highest possible good, humanity lost the faithful certainty of God's presence. No longer perceiving God in what was once faithful certainty, they and their descendants perceived instead, in angst, God's apparent absence. Seeking knowledge of non-being and finding it to be nothing, they gained anxiety by excluding themselves from intimate converse with Being.

> From now on, anxiety is intrinsic to the mind on the basis of the gaping void in it, but this immanence has a transcendent prerequisite: alienation from God. Thus, "Nothing" is the proximate basis for anxiety, but the nothing that makes anxiety anxious is not simply the nothingness that pervades finitude as such, the mind's inner transcendence and contingency. Rather, what makes anxiety anxious is the awareness of a fundamental falsehood, displacement, guilt—an awareness called forth by the absence of the One who ought to be present in this "Nothing."[51]

The "nothing" Kierkegaard says "begets anxiety"[52] is rather for Balthasar the "nothingness that pervades finitude as such, the mind's inner transcendence and contingency."[53] The nothing that makes us anxious stems from our unconscious sense of the wrongness of felt guilt caused by God's apparent absence from our hearts, that is, from the space originally created for the divine presence to abide.

No longer spiritually certain of our relationship with the creator, the human heart has instead sought certainty in the only alternative: the crowded creation in which we abide. As a palliative to the aching emptiness within, we seek absolute certainty in finitude, in sensory "data" gleaned from the circumscriptions of the human sensorium and intellect. The wonders open to the senses have instead informed human experience through an unrequited hunger for apparently lost certainty. Through the ages and until the present time, this good consequence of Adam's sin

51. Balthasar, *The Christian and Anxiety*, 142.

52. Kierkegaard, *Concept of Anxiety*, 41.

53. Balthasar, *The Christian and Anxiety*, 142.

led to constant creative advances and enhancement of human life. In short, Original Sin has led to science in the broadest sense of the latter's meaning. Great good has come out of primordial evil. Throughout it all, the place in the human heart created by God for divine repose has seemed empty and dark: the locus of divine abandonment and the root of the pain of exclusion we experience at all stages of human life, from childhood to adulthood, throughout aging and unto death. *All* life's exclusions harmonize with this primordial exclusion-experience of apparent abandonment.

Freedom's Hope: Christ's Redemption

And yet God did *not* abandon us in reality, else our very being would have abruptly ended in the puff of nothing. Adam instead chose to seek to know. As we have seen, who and what we are finds its origin and essence in God. As embodied spirit, we are infinitely more than we sense and think. Yet we are limited by provenance. God resides still, as always, in the heart of our being, as the very ground of who and what we are. God is still and always there, although we sense a dark emptiness rather than the clarity that was Adam's before his fall: the blindness of faithful sight now lost. Balthasar again:

> Anxiety arrived on the scene with the void, and Christ's redemption does not eliminate this void. His redemption, to be sure, brings God's fullness, but it conveys it into the form of this void. It is said of the Redeemer that he emptied himself and made his way into the void.[54]

God created Adam and Eve to be possessed of the original faithful certainty they would subsequently cast off. Human nature was so marred by the aspiration to become divine that God humbled it, denying the first man and woman the clarity of undoubting faith. The greatest longing of the human heart is to recover some semblance of our original certainty, albeit unconsciously. We can do so in prayer, entreating God to grant full restoration to us of the

54. Balthasar, *The Christian and Anxiety*, 142–43.

original faith of Adam. Or we can seek it by our own efforts in the fullest knowledge-embrace of this world that we can accomplish.

Living incomplete existences without full assurance of God's intimacy, we seek to know ourselves in the world at hand through our senses—consolation for the apparent emptiness within. Yet the fullness of that consolation is always just out of reach, hidden in the kenosis that is the quality of God's ongoing self-revelation. This is the cause of all human suffering. But we are not alone in this darkness. In his Incarnation as a human being, the Redeemer attained experience of human life without sin. Jesus, taking on the anxiety of all humanity, also experienced the pain of separation from the Father, as revealed in his cry of abandonment on the cross. Balthasar deduces that "only the Son knows exhaustively what it means to be forsaken by the Father, for he alone knows who the Father is and what the Father's intimacy and love are."[55] Jesus took on all human anxiety and redeemed it:

> Ever since the Lord's expiatory suffering on the Cross, in which he made the anxiety of each and every sin—indeed, the oneness of the whole world's anxiety—merge into the oneness of his anxiety as God-Man, an isolated penance for an isolated, personal guilt is, for a Christian, no longer conceivable.[56]

Yet even in redemption, we have not been fully restored to Adam's original intimacy with divine presence. We are assured, as a people, of Christ's presence in the sacraments of the church and through the proclamation of Scripture. But we are still denied primordial intimacy. We can only imagine what it was like. In communal retrospect, Balthasar waxes poetic about how Adam's consolation might have felt:

> In the evening breeze of paradise God walks and talks with Adam: invisible, yet as tangible and all-pervasive as the wind. In him we live, and move, and have our being.[57]

55. Balthasar, *The Christian and Anxiety*, 75.

56. Balthasar, *The Christian and Anxiety*, 92.

57. Balthasar, *The Christian and Anxiety*, 135.

Anxiety remains "something general and neutral, a basic given of human existence as such."[58] The void remains, yet "God's fullness reveals itself as presence in such a way that God as the first thing demands from man a total Yes to his invisible totality and in-difference."[59] Elijah heard the consolation of God only in a tiny whispering sound.[60] The challenge of faith is to listen to the living Word and believe without empirical verification beyond the shared witness of the Holy Spirit.

> The void is thereby filled, to be sure: God is there. But he is no longer there in the way he was present in the evening breeze of paradise—as that Presence which, for man and his nature, is the most real, in which and through which everything else gains its reality. Instead God is present as the unfelt fullness, as fullness in the void.[61]

In the present day, we have inherited the only certainty of God available to us: in the sacraments, in tradition, in Scripture, and in the subjective consolation of faith-shared experience. These must suffice for us as fullness in the void. In the unity of eucharistic worship, Christ is tangibly present in sensory experience—our earthly share in the heavenly banquet. Only after Christ returns and we rise again with him, and sit at table assembled in the divine presence, shall our original intimacy with God be fully restored.

58. Balthasar, *The Christian and Anxiety*, 40.

59. Balthasar, *The Christian and Anxiety*, 143.

60. 1 Kgs 19:13.

61. Balthasar, *The Christian and Anxiety*, 142–43.

On Creation

In the early 1960s, Karl Rahner established parameters to clarify how the Catholic position on evolution was harmonious with that of science. He sought to show that a balanced, rational dialogue between theologians and scientists is possible as long as both parties recognize the integrity of each other's methodologies. Rahner's efforts helped interrupt the apparent impasse in the discussion that had been in evidence for the better part of the century following the publication of Charles Darwin's groundbreaking study.

According to Catholic teaching, there is no contradiction between the truth of creation and the theory of evolution.[1] Indeed, historically, the Catholic Church has maintained tolerance toward the theory.[2] The 1909 edition of the *Catholic Encyclopedia* states

1. In a personal letter to a fellow Oratorian in 1868, John Henry Newman makes perhaps the earliest formulation of evolutionary theory in relation to Christian thought: "If Mr. Darwin in this or that point of his theory comes into collision with revealed truth, that is another matter—but I do not see that the *principle* of development, or what I have called construction, does . . . Mr. Darwin's theory *need* not then . . . be atheistical, be it true or not; it may simply be suggesting a larger idea of Divine Prescience and Skill . . . [A]nd I do not [see] that 'the accidental evolution of organic beings' is inconsistent with divine design—It is accidental to *us*, not to *God*." Newman, *Letters and Diaries*, 77–78.

2. It was the Church of England who initially opposed the theory. Although there are no surviving transcripts, according to summary reports published in journals such as *The Guardian*, *The Athenaeum*, and *Jackson's Oxford Journal*, Bishop Wilberforce debated Thomas Huxley on the theory of evolution in June 1860. See Thomson, "Marginalia," 210–13.

Other theologians, however, sought to integrate theology and evolution on

that evolution is "in perfect agreement with the Christian conception of the universe."[3] For Catholic theology, the crucial qualification has always been that the human soul cannot be the product of purely material processes. Notwithstanding the human body's evolution from other forms of life, *the human soul*, the Church teaches, *is God's direct creation.*

In 1951, Pope Pius XII formalized the doctrine of the creation of the soul, welcoming investigations of the evolution of the human body as long as they did not insist on atheistic conclusions. Recognizing that God may have employed evolutionary means to effect ongoing creation represents no necessary contradiction to faith, Pius XII explained. Cosmogenesis *is* creation.

Drawing upon the writings of Rahner and others, what follows is a consideration of Catholic theology's resonance with the theory of evolution, a resonance that is less juridical than it is inspired by recognition of God's self-revelation in creating and redeeming the universe.

Let us begin with the theory in question.

Evolution in a Nutshell

Evolutionary theory was a by-product of nineteenth-century thinking. It did not spring spontaneously into the minds of Charles Darwin and Alfred Wallace, but rather extended from philosophical speculations by other scholars and naturalists from the previous century. In the eighteenth century, a static model of the cosmos was prevalent. One hundred years later, the idea of *development through processes of incremental change* not only captivated the natural sciences, but permeated philosophy, theology, history, and the humanities (particularly psychology) as well.

---

the basis of theosophical accounts of emergent order, the birth of God from the unground, etc. It seems the theosophical accounts of emergent order in fact preceded the natural scientific accounts—by a century at least. See Benz, *Evolution and Christian Hope*, 64–71.

3. Wasmann, "Catholics and Evolution," para. 2.

Although first proposed by Wallace, Darwin formulated evolution as a scientific theory in two books, *The Origin of Species* (1859) and *The Descent of Man* (1871). The theory is predicated on the principle of change over time—specifically, that living species derive from earlier forms of related species. With the development of paleontology in the eighteenth century, the exhumation of fossils of species no longer extant (in the absence of fossils of modern species alongside them) gave credence to the suggestion that living things today evolved to their present form over the course of millions of years.

Darwin's theory contrasted with Jean-Baptiste Lamarck's in that Darwin posited that the process of evolution advanced *incrementally* and was driven by environmental changes that selected for individuals capable of surviving those changes over those incapable of surviving them. Lamarck before him had proposed that individual creatures experienced changes in their bodily form during their lifetime and subsequently passed those changes on to their offspring. Darwin's presumption, in contrast, was that if species possessed naturally occurring advantages, those advantages would be inherited, whereas individuals of the same species who had not inherited such advantages would die. Thus, in a process Darwin would call "natural selection," fewer and fewer disadvantaged individuals would reproduce over time, allowing for the flourishing and continuation of more advantageous traits.

Natural selection did not become the sole dynamic accepted as a driver of the evolutionary process, however. In the early twentieth century, alternative mechanisms such as spontaneous genetic mutation were proposed. Modern theory has melded together these two mechanisms—natural selection and genetic mutation—and, despite there being problems with both mechanisms,[4] evolu-

4. "The majority of genetic mutations are detrimental, making both genetic mutation and natural selection too slow to account for the rapid emergence of new species after so-called extinction events in the remote past. What should have taken millions of years has in some cases occurred over the course of thousands.

"Rapid recovery after an extinction event comes through surviving species, who fill available ecological niches. Full recovery takes as long as ten million

tion (although not yet fully characterized) is generally accepted today as the means by which new species of life emerge.

The Causal Principles Determining Evolution and Creation

Evolution and creation can be reconciled by illuminating the causal principle that is operative in each. One can study *that* things exist at all as well as *how* they came to be in time. Theologically speaking, that things exist depends upon their ultimate source in God. Insofar as God is subject neither to time's passage nor to material change, divine intentionality does not change over time. Rather, it is the other way around: as Augustine reminds us, time is the first of God's creatures, predating heaven and earth.[5] From the perspective of science, on the other hand, how things exist or come to be depends on sequences of incremental, causally connected events that unfold over time.

Everything we experience in human life unfolds within our perception of time. Theology reminds us that we are reliant in every moment of our existence on God, who is the source and sustenance of all that we are in time. Divine providence maintains us in existence, in a being-dialogue with God.

Thus, evolution can be thought through in light of creation given the following:

1. God is the ultimate source of creation of the cosmos.
2. Evolution is a possible efficient means of bringing about God's creation in time.

---

years of further evolution because it takes that long to recover the genetic diversity lost through the extinction event." University of Texas at Austin, "Evolution imposes 'speed limit' on recovery after mass extinctions," *ScienceDaily*.

5. "And if time began to be together with heaven and earth, no time can be found in which God had not made heaven and earth." Augustine, "On Genesis," *The Works of Saint Augustine*, 41.

The *Logos*

When we seek truth, either in the everyday world or in theoretical intellectual pursuits, we expect that the universe will make sense. The name for this expectation of reasonableness is *logos*, the grounding presupposition underlying every possible question. The universe makes sense, and the laws that unify it are discoverable by observation and the processes of deduction and induction. Even though the scientific method is limited to sensory data, it presumes, much like theology presumes, a unity about the organization of the material universe that cannot be directly sensed within the time frame of human existence. Despite remaining a problem, metaphysics is inescapable.

Even though theological insights into truth are extraneous to the scientific method, both theology and science are grounded in a basic belief in universal reason. Though the purview of science is limited to what can be sensed, theology is not so confined. Herein lies the crucial difference between the *logos* of science and the *Logos* of faith.

Scientific *logos* is the rational principle grounding all truth. In contrast, divine *Logos* is divine truth—the source of all created truth. The *logos* of science is not identical to the *Logos* of theology, although historically they derive from a common *ratio*.[6] The scientist non-believer need not do so, but a faithful believer can hold both forms of *logos* to be true.

Ratio is essential to faith. The Book of Wisdom relates that the wisdom or reason of God was present when the world was created. The theology of Christ's presence at creation is mirrored in the New Testament in Paul's letters, and it is what the first chapter of John's Gospel addresses: "In the beginning was the Word (*Logos*), and the Word was with God, and the Word was God" (John 1:1). The difference between the reason of the world, the *logos* that

6. Augustine saw *ratio* as "the mind's capacity of distinguishing and connecting the things that are learned." For Augustine, *ratio* "precedes the exercise of the intellectual capacity." Rolbiecki, "Ratio," *Dictionary of Philosophy*.

unifies all created truth, and the uncreated reason and wisdom of God, is that divine *Logos* is a divine person.

The ancient Greeks never conceived of *logos* as a person, and it must have shocked their descendants to hear it avowed by Christians in such terms. That the reasonableness of the world finds its origin, its ultimate cause, in divine reason is a Christian faith statement—a presupposition grounded in conviction sourced in divine revelation. Theologically speaking, *logos* is created. Divine *Logos* is the uncreated Son, the Word of God made flesh, who, in reason, created the world of time, space, and perceptible beings therein.

Mercifully, the Catholic Church can no longer insist that science toe the line of dogma. However, scientists continue to draw conclusions about theology and faith that take them too far away from the presuppositions enabling their professional methods. Science, after all, lacks methodological access to the transcendent. If unicorns do not exist, how could the scientific method prove this definitively beyond a skeptical statement of belief? "Absence of proof is not proof of absence" was a principle established by Sextus Empiricus as fundamental to the skeptic and thus to the scientific method. Some scientists have forgotten the limits of their discipline and have declared God's absence to be a fact of scientific truth. Methodologically, however, this cannot be.

The challenge for the evolution debate is for each side to be more aware of its fundamental ground—to distinguish between the objects peculiar to each discipline and acknowledge the objects they have in common.

Problems of Terminology

Dialogue between science and theology is possible if we first establish common terminology.

Some scientific terms have a meaning that is not precisely matched by their theological cognates. Take the word *random*, for example. The process of evolution, according to some interpretations, is determined by the exigencies of "random chance."[7] As we have seen, the mainspring of modern evolutionary theory is that natural selection acts upon random genetic variations.

Theologically speaking, there is nothing random about God's intention to create. God created all in love, perpetually and decisively, for the sake of establishing a loving relationship with creatures, most especially those created in the divine image and likeness. To claim that God's intention was random in the colloquial sense of the word would render creation the work of a scatterbrain. It is necessary, therefore, to establish correspondence between the scientific and theological meanings of the word *random*: theologically, *random* means "unplanned" or "unguided"; scientifically, *random* possesses quite different connotations.

In 2005, Stephen M. Barr, a theoretical particle physicist from the University of Delaware, clarified apparent misunderstandings that had arisen following an article written by Cardinal Schönborn on evolution.[8] Barr argued that scientists never use the words *unplanned* or *unguided* in reference to evolution. The *Science Citation Index* for that year listed only forty-eight scientific papers mentioning *unguided* in the title, most of them to do with missiles. Only 467 papers contained the word *unplanned*, almost all to do with pregnancies and medical procedures. In contrast, there were 52,633 papers with *random* in the title from all other areas of scientific research.

In science, *random* is used to denote a quality of statistical dynamics—for example, the movement of atomic or molecular particles in a gas, or subatomic particle fluctuations in quantum fields, or the recombination of genes in the process of meiotic cell division.[9] *Random* in these contexts does not mean uncaused

7. This is in spite of the fact that chaos theory has cast into doubt whether true randomness is manifest in natural phenomena.

8. Barr, "The Evolution of Design," 9–12. Stephen M. Barr, "The Evolution of Design," *First Things*, 156 (October 2005): 9–12.

9. The position of a gene on a chromosome during the process of meiosis determines its ability to "cross over" to the recombined DNA strand. The closer the gene is to the telomere, the more likely crossing over takes place. The closer the gene is to the centromere, the less likely crossing over will occur.

or unplanned; rather, it means "statistically uncorrelated." To illustrate this difference, Barr offers the example of a typical game played by his children in their family car. In the game, they call out the origin of passing cars as given by the car's license plates. The sequence of states or provinces of origin is sufficiently random for the children to be unable to accurately predict the next car's origin. The origins of the cars are uncorrelated. Yet, each car is where it is, in that sequence, at that time, *for a reason*. Each reason is peculiar to the intentions of the driver and thus beyond the capacity of the scientific method to determine.

Barr's license-plate game illustrates the persistent problem of using statistics to analyze human behavior. The assumption of randomness in statistical theory collides with the assumption of the purposiveness of human action. It illustrates that an action can be both random and purposive simultaneously. Correspondingly, it is needless to reject out of hand the premise that random activity in the process of gene recombination that eventually leads to species change—to evolution—is a possible means by which God directs perpetual creation. Evolution could be both purposive and scientifically random without exclusion or contradiction. The unfolding of evolution should not be too difficult for an omnipotent creator with infinite knowledge and infinite capacity for loving and giving. Again, the scientific method cannot conclusively rule out this possibility.

Yet those who universally reject evolution avoid this issue, effectively denying its scientific validity by maintaining that *random* means unguided, choosing the colloquial meaning to undermine the scientific one. This error stems either from a lack of scientific literacy or from fraudulent practitioners who know better but have ulterior motives. If there is a contradiction between creation and evolution, it does not reside in "science versus religion," but in the misuse of language for rhetorical and political purposes.

Genes directly adjacent to the centromere never cross over. Thus, there is no inherent mechanism in the meiotic process that would justify randomness in the willy-nilly sense.

The problem is not which side is right or wrong, but a lack of recognition of methodological limits. The church in the seventeenth century overstepped theological method and made dogmatic statements about the natural world with unjustifiable consequences. As for scientists, it is ironic when atheists among them conclude that evolution cannot be God-intended, drawing a theological rather than scientific conclusion. If God is not a possible scientific object, divine intention cannot be falsifiable. Atheism, no less than theism, is based on the cogitative process of belief.

Truth can only be disclosed in a dialogue in which each participant co-intends promoting understanding. For believers in the Incarnation, because the risen Jesus Christ is God-with-us, the *Logos* of God infinitely indwells the world, providentially generating the *logos*. True debate has the *logos*, the presumption of reasonableness, as its common ground, whether you accept the capitalized version of the word or not.

Rahner and Evolution

Having clarified the theory and terminology in question, let us examine how Karl Rahner establishes parameters within which the Catholic position on evolution can be seen in its harmony with science. First, he discusses the presuppositions of faith upon which he will base his arguments. God, who is "absolute spirit, pure meaning, intelligibility, and love," *created everything that is not God*. "Everything that is, therefore, must bear the stamp of origin of this one primordial ground of being; everything must have an ultimate unity and community."[10] God is the source of the unity of our common existence.

Second, Rahner affirms that human existence is, in nature, *spiritual*, "which manifests itself in intelligibility." Rather than reaffirming the spirit–body dichotomy, he affirms that materiality originates from the creative action of Spirit. The spiritual

10. Rahner, "Natural Science and Reasonable Faith," *Theological Investigations*, vol. 21, 34.

physicality of the human person is ontologically inseparable. Science cannot verify this presupposition, of course, because materiality is all that science considers; spirit is beyond its ken. Rahner nonetheless recognizes it as integral to theology; crucially, if matter were completely other than spirit, it could not be "conceived of as originating from an absolute spirit, since this spirit cannot create something that is absolutely disparate from itself."[11] This is why the Gnostics thought of matter as evil, concluding it to be the creation of the evil force of the universe, with spirit being the creation of the force of good. The Gnostics imagined the cosmos as a "duel" between opposite forces rather than the singular creation of an infinite God. In positing matter as the lowest form of *spirit*, we can see in the individual the unity of body and soul, and in the community of diverse individuals the unity of being in God.

> [I]f we must assume an ultimately intelligible relationship of the individual realities of the world, then this relationship of the individual realities to one another cannot be conceived as anything but final, that is, as an interrelationship that has been ultimately intended and planned.[12]

The relationship of the material reality of the body to spirit, and of individual humans to humanity as a whole, are final realities. This finality inheres in being in a state of constancy in relationship despite undergoing constant change. It links every existent thing to the divine source of existence. The innumerable causes and effects that bring about changes in life once we come into being do not change the finality of the relationship things have to each other and to God. *Finality itself is not limited by our ability to understand God, who is ultimately unintelligible.* Rahner shows us that questions of *what* and *that* are inextricably linked.

Although linked to God, we are, crucially, separate beings. Created being has an autonomy that ensures individuality and distinction from God, who is infinitely Other. If God were an element

11. Rahner, *Theological Investigations*, vol. 21, 34–35.

12. Rahner, *Theological Investigations*, vol. 21, 35.

of creation—that is, if created beings were somehow *constituent components* of the creator—it would mean two things:

1. God would be limited to and identical with created being.
2. The unique being of each individual thing would be merely a constituent of God's being, hence not unique at all.

Given the foregoing, what we *could* know about God would already be part of who and what we are. In a pantheistic universe, therefore, we could study the rest of creation and eventually learn all there is to know about it *and* God. We would not be free individually, and God would be the thrall of his own creation—which is the very definition of sin.[13]

Rahner uses the incongruities of the pantheistic model of God to establish the necessity of revelation. If God is completely Other than we are and not a constituent part of the universe (or the entire universe *per se*), but rather its origin and sustenance, and *we* possess *independent* being, then the only way we can know of God is if God reveals his divinity to us. For a pantheistic God, in contrast, revelation would correspond directly with creation itself.

> [D]ivine causality does not presuppose the distinction between God and creature, but itself establishes this distinction and precisely in so doing keeps it within itself in a unique way . . . [T]he determination and events of a finite being are subject to the constant "pressure" of the divine being. This "pressure" is not one of the essential constitutive elements of a finite being. It can, however, always make this being into something more than it is

13. Limited human freedom is contingent on God's infinite freedom. Sin is rejection of God's transcendence and the self-elevating of ours. In a pantheistic universe, God would not be transcendent, but rather universally immanent, because everything existing would *be* God. Hence, God's supremacy would be lowered to that of any other non-transcendent being. If so, we would be component parts of God, co-limited by a common unfreedom: like unto God. However, in a universe created by a transcendent God, such a contention is a contradiction and a denial of convenience justifying moral license. It is the sin of Adam. Adam was the first pantheist. He could not be equal to God unless he dragged God down a peg or two.

> "in itself". . . [I]t is that which in the first place makes the finite being what it is.[14]

The pressure Rahner speaks of is the ongoing act of creation. For a transcendent God, creation is a preparatory necessity of revelation's possibility. Thus, because God is infinite, revelation through creation is never-ending, always waxing.

One of the peculiarities of the theory of evolution is that *it observes more coming out of less*. This observation does not contradict Catholic theology, which teaches that God created us to be capable of becoming more through the pressure of uncreated grace. In other words, theologically speaking, our nature can be increased by the same supernatural source of grace that made us in the first place. Such an increase is not extraneous, but the continuation of a process already ongoing from the beginning, synonymous with generation.

Yet not all being is discernable to the senses. If evolution from a scientific perspective describes a continuous increase of being in the expanding cosmos and living biosphere, and science cannot account for that increase except to say that it is the result of a process that is statistically uncorrelated, we must acknowledge and abide by that conclusion of science as correct within its methodologically limited purview. But as we have seen, the theory of evolution is *congruent with a theology that recognizes increase*—more coming from less. It is consistent with the definition of creation itself, that is, with God's constantly sustaining presence in existence nurturing the flourishing of all that is. From this standpoint, the theory of evolution is consistent with both scientific method and the traditional theology of revelation.

The Problem of Hominization in Evolutionary Terms

If evolution has its source in God as its ultimate cause, then because it is a natural process, and nature finds its increase in grace, God must have endowed each living thing with an intrinsic potency to

14. Rahner, *Theological Investigations*, vol. 21, 36–37.

actualize independently according to its natural attributes (we call this *secondary causality*). We have seen that the evolutionary process cannot be fully apparent to science. For Rahner, this is given, evidence that the transcendental relationship between absolute being and finite being is one that "precedes any application of a general principle of causality."[15] For theology, this transcendental relationship between creation and God *must* be prior to any discovered datum of natural science. Hidden in the essence of matter is unreachable evidence of God's creative power. What becomes evident to us in the disclosure of being flows from the eternality hidden in its interiority. The transcendental relationship of the absolute to the finite is *not* an on-switch for being as such, but is extant "always and everywhere" as an ongoing relationship between the two—*the means by which becoming persists*. Most importantly, it is a "determination of self-transcendence coming from absolute being itself."[16] Hence, the becoming-more that is the act of being-thus is the *fundamental nature of created being* emerging through grace into disclosure from its hidden essence, under the pressure of absolute being. The only way a being can become more is to first have the potential for it—a potential that is the characteristic emergent quality of its becoming in the universe.

As we have seen, science recognizes that more comes from less—in the ongoing reality of universal inflation[17] and in the biological evolutionary process that is one of its constituent modes. Again, scientific observation of the universe does not contradict the theological view that it is in the nature of beings to transcend themselves. In the case of being human, we might add that it is through God's grace that we are transformed as individuals and as a people. But this does not address the problem of the biological evolution of consciousness. Greater even than the problem of life emerging from the abiotic universe is the problem of consciousness

15. Rahner, *Theological Investigations*, vol. 21, 39.

16. Rahner, *Theological Investigations*, vol. 21, 39.

17. Although, as the universe inflates, even as it may not gain mass, its dimensions increase. However, it is also possible that, if creation is ongoing, mass may be continuously added. The term "inflation" remains adequate.

leading to the fullness of created self-awareness, expressed as the free and rational choice of human spirit.

Hans Urs von Balthasar asserts that the distinguishing quality of self-reflective being is that it encloses an infinite intimacy within possessed of the freedom to disclose or withhold itself. How did self-awareness evolve from purely sensate life, through the various stages of consciousness, to achieve this intimate, volitional sapience in human life?

Clearly, hominization was a speciation[18] event and could not have been biologically derived from a single mating pair. When we briefly put aside purely mythological explanations, we conclude that hominization was a biological process by which a significant genetic population became stabilized into a viable reproductive agency whereby species-level genetic vigor became established over a long period of time. Let us imagine that, one-half million years ago, a population of advanced hominins—our immediate biological ancestors—reached the biological potential to exist in unity with a soul. This pre-human form would still have had an animal soul, possessed of a simple finite reality that would, according to dogma, cease to exist upon its death. The hominization event presumably occurred after this pre-human form reached this biological potential.

In view of secondary causality, how can we conceive of hominization as possible without theorizing the human soul as an external supplement to the physical essence of the human body? Along such lines, the creature's essence would remain material and the "addition" of a soul would become an accidental quality of its material essence. In this model, such activity would represent an interruption. Rahner speculates: "Does this not postulate an event in which secondary causes within the closed causal series are suddenly replaced by God himself? Does that not make God a demiurge?"[19] Any intervention must be God's direct activity, or else the doctrinal position that the human soul does not derive

18. Speciation is the evolutionary formation of a new species over time.

19. Rahner, *Hominisation*, 66.

from universal inflation would be violated, and God would be demoted to the level of effecting secondary cause.

How can the soul, which is an essential property of being human, not be an "add-on" but rather the embodiment of new creation? The matter has been the source of considerable doctrinal controversy.

The Problem of Hominization in Doctrinal Terms

Plato thought the soul pre-existed the body in a "not-here" ideal world. The human being on earth, a world of mere shadow, was a soul trapped in matter that retained innate knowledge of and from its pre-existence. In the third century of the Christian era, Origen advanced a theory of the pre-existence of souls that he derived from Neo-Platonism. Many Church Fathers in the two centuries that followed, including Gregory of Nyssa,[20] Jerome,[21] and Augustine,[22] firmly rejected this doctrine as false. Following Aristotle, Thomas Aquinas later thought the unity of body and soul was self-evident. We cannot be human with just a mind without a body

> because it is one and the same man who is conscious both that he understands and that he senses. But one cannot sense without a body, and therefore the body must be some part of man.[23]

Minds alone cannot have a full experience of human life. If the soul were to pre-exist the body, then it could not be human. The pre-existence of the human soul was thus rejected throughout the history of orthodox Christian thought. The consensus in the tradition has been that the only created souls without bodies were

20. See Nyssa, *On the Making of Man*, in Schaff and Wace, *Nicene and Post-Nicene Fathers*, vol. 5, 419–20.

21. See Jerome, *Apology against Rufinus*, book I, para. 15.

22. See Augustine, *City of God*, in Schaff, *Nicene and Post-Nicene Fathers*, vol. 2, 245.

23. Aquinas, *Summa Theologiae*, part 1, question 76, 555.

those of angels.[24] If we were to speculate that a human body suddenly became ready to "take on" a soul at the hominization event, our inquiry would be at variance with both traditions.

How do we reconcile the acceptance of evolutionary theory by the encyclical *Humani generis* with the tacit rejection of the pre-existent soul by the Fathers of the Church? Pius XII accepted "the doctrine of evolutionism" "in so far as it inquires into the origin of the human body, that is to say the living matter of the progeny is derived from the above . . . [and] created immediately by God"[25] Human procreation is the co-creative act of human birth parents and God, each contributing to the child's created essence. By analogy, in the evolution of the pre-human being into the human being, we can neither consider the soul to have been a secondary addition to a pre-evolved body, nor the body to have been necessarily and sufficiently evolved to render it capable of accommodating a pre-existent soul. The unity of the human body and soul as one substance would not be preserved in either case.[26]

It is clear from our analysis that the reality of the human entry into the biotic universe must be "a truly new, original and different kind of reality, and not . . . something derivative,"[27] that is, unlike any previous speciation event. In no way are we suggesting, however, that the human race bypassed secondary causation and descended body and soul from the sky in a chariot to become a part of Earth's biota as a special creation—a suggestion critics

24. Angels are not, and never have been, and never can in any way become human. Hollywood constantly portrays story premises of angels losing their wings and falling to earth as human. It is heretical nonsense.

25. ". . . '*evolutionismi*' *doctrina, quatenus nempe de humani corporis origine inquirit ex iam exsistente ac vivente materia oriundi—animas enim a Deo immediate creari catholica fides nos retinere iubet.*" Pope Pius XII, *Humani Generis*, para. 36.

26. Ensoulment in the evolution of the first humans could have been accomplished in the same way as in procreation—*de novo* at the birth of the first human being. However, this would mean the first parents were not human, which is not scriptural and would present an even greater theological problem.

27. Rahner, *Hominisation*, 20.

incorrectly perceive to be central to Christian dogma. Rahner states the correction eloquently:

> The original doctrine of faith . . . is that man comes from the earth, that the whole man is concerned in this origin of his, which is at least "also" one of his sources. At any rate his material origin is a determining factor that affects the whole man.[28]

As have all other living things, humanity comes from the earth—not merely bodily, as have other beings, but as *embodied spirit*. Humanity's union with spirit is effected by God on earth, not delivered by divine courier from heaven. Encumbered as we are by the Platonic idea that the human body is merely a vestment that our soul puts on, Christian teaching consistently asserts that the human "soul is not a thing on its own, which at any given moment can exist or be understood really independently of a relation to matter, but is the name of one component in the inner complexity of the one human being."[29] Further complicating this matter is the church's teaching that the nature of soul in contrast to body is determined by fundamental differences between spirit and matter. Rahner continues:

> In connection with the question of the evolutionary origins of man, the Church's teaching emphasizes that spirit and matter are not the same, that spirit cannot be derived from matter, and that man, because spiritual, has a metaphysically irreducible position in the cosmos, so that his origin, as far as his spiritual nature is concerned, cannot be found in matter.[30]

Even as matter itself ultimately finds its origin in God, so too must there be a causal principle—qualitative of each human being—accordant with God cogenerating the soul with the body into an integral human essence. All contingent beings are capable of attaining transcendence from their current state, a capacity obtained in the

28. Rahner, *Hominisation*, 23.
29. Rahner, *Hominisation*, 23.
30. Rahner, *Hominisation*, 46.

first watershed event in cosmological evolution: the emergence of life from abiotic matter. All living beings have souls proper to their state. But *human* souls are uniquely *spiritual* and therefore eternal, which is the breakthrough of the second watershed event. The third,[31] the Incarnation, was actuated by the power of the Holy Spirit when a divine person united with human nature: the intrinsic unity of human soul and human body with divine being.

Rahner's "Christology within an Evolutionary View"

Each agent in the cosmos fulfills its creative potential because God intended its particular qualities. By its act of existence, each creature fulfills a particular divine intention in its act of continuous becoming. Each particularity, added to all other particularities, is the summed potency and driving force in cosmogenesis throughout the history of the universe. Humans participate in a special way in this action, but not as merely extant beings (like abiotic matter), or in biotic sub-sagacity (like nonhuman life). Humans reflect upon life, upon who we are and what we do, willfully orienting ourselves toward God, our source and endpoint, via the *same* human nature through which God revealed the Son to us. The uniqueness of each human life is a *gift-self*, God-given and God-chosen to fulfill a divine purpose.

In hominization, a human soul was empowered freely to act physically—to choose or not choose self-determinately. This gift of freedom made us human. As freely intending self-reflecting spirits, humans have consciously contributed to cosmogenesis.[32] Hominization rendered the cosmos anthropocentric because human consciousness brought non-sapient unity to self-awareness of

31. Though drawn from an understanding of evolution inspired by Catholic theology, the term "watershed event," and the coinage of these three watershed moments, is my own.

32. This presumption of human uniqueness is likely very presumptuous. It depends upon no other self-reflecting spirits existing in a universe with literally trillions of Earth-like planets on which life could have evolved. Statistically, there most certainly must be nonhuman embodied spirits dwelling within such vastness.

the cosmos through ensouled cognition of its sapient constituents. This anthropocentrism does not devalue the nonhuman cosmos; rather, it represents the embodiment of its breakthrough into transcendence. In creating the human soul's inextricable integrity with its body, God "othered" humanity into being, our unique evolution from matter and energy mysteriously ensouling us directly.

Rahner wrote an essay in the early sixties entitled "Christology within an Evolutionary View." In it, he coined the term "active self-transcendence" to characterize the amalgam of natural and divine causation in the hominization event. For hominization to have occurred, matter had to be predisposed to accommodating the divine ingress in the Incarnation. In light of this, Rahner affirms the predisposition of matter to move toward spirit:

> Starting from this inner interrelation between these two factors and concentrating on the temporal duration of this relationship between these two factors, it may be said without scruple that matter develops out of its inner being in the direction of the spirit.[33]

The predisposition of created being, therefore, is to move ever toward perfection, toward spirit, a movement it cannot accomplish of itself, as we have seen, because it moves toward an inaccessible Other. Biotic being, endowed with vegetative and animal soul-attributes, moves ever toward rational spirit but never achieves it, except when God draws it toward himself, transforming the merely natural into the supernatural likeness of God. In the etiology of the Garden, the embodied human spirit that aspired to be like God failed because created being cannot willfully transcend toward the creator without first being drawn.[34] Human being is the embodied spirit of self-awareness, and the othering we experience *as* experience results from an ongoing gift of grace. Grace maintains us in

33. Rahner, "Christology Within an Evolutionary View," *Theological Investigations*, vol. 5, 164.

34. Attempts to "force" the *Parousia* through neglect of the world are a modern residue of the Fall.

existence and saves us from flawed willfulness, thus enabling us to choose rightly if we so intend it.[35]

Divine providence is not merely graced sufficiency that diligently "tops up" our being, keeping it from being-dissipation. Built into the fabric of all contingent being, moreover, is the potency to become more than merely *this*. The very nature of our being is becoming, a pre-charged orientation toward transcendence.

> First of all, if there is any 'becoming' at all . . . then 'becoming' in its true form cannot be conceived simply as a 'becoming other' in which a reality becomes different but does not become more. True 'becoming' must be conceived as something 'becoming more,' as the coming into being of more reality, as an effective attainment of a greater fullness of being. This 'more' must not be imagined, however, as something simply added to what was there before, but, on the one hand, must be something really effected by what was there before and, on the other hand, must be the inner increase of being proper to the previously existing reality. This means, however, that if it is really to be taken seriously, 'becoming' must be understood as a real self-transcendence, a surpassing of self or active filling up of the empty.[36]

In the intimate interiority of being that yet remains undisclosed, "becoming more" can be disclosed, at any point in a being's existence, out of the potency inscribed in its essence. In the case of individual human becoming, this willed act alone cannot account for the process by which hominization occurred. The Holy Spirit indwelling the universe plays a creative part in the ongoing creation that is cosmogenesis. As Rahner explains, "this notion of self-transcendence includes also transcendence into what is substantially new, i.e., the leap to a higher *nature*."[37] This is how human being is the fulfillment of the potency of material becoming in the cosmos. In the second cosmic watershed of hominization—in

35. Process thought struggles with grace, because God bottles it up, not intervening in creation.

36. Rahner, *Theological Investigations*, vol. 5, 164.

37. Rahner, *Theological Investigations*, vol. 5, 165.

the final phase of cosmic othering—living matter broke through into becoming, like God in its eternal human soul, but *wholly other* than God in its materiality. We are unlike any other created being we know of. However, even the human soul is other than God—contingent, not necessary; created, not empyreal—through the agency of God's infinite divine spirit. Cosmological inflation, which includes evolution, is the process of continuous othering through the agency of God's graced impetus.

God's othering of Earth's motley embodied spirits was not an artifact of divine bisociation, like a chef combining old recipes to stew up a new *plat du jour*.[38] The singular paradox about being created human is that we were othered *as God's image and likeness*, hence unlike any other creature. About God's capping of the cosmos thus, Rahner offers this crucial point, which is actually the culminating point of all:

> God does not merely create something other than himself—he also gives himself to this other. The world received God, the Infinite and the ineffable mystery, to such an extent that he himself becomes its innermost life. The concentrated, always unique self-possession of the cosmos in each individual spiritual person, and in his transcendence towards the absolute ground of his reality, takes place when this absolute ground itself becomes directly interior to that which is grounded by it.[39]

The cosmos came into being as a willed act of divine self-revelation. Its enactment instituted God's ongoing revelation, which ultimately reached fullness in the Incarnation—in the union of God's Word with Jesus's human embodied spirit. Creation was an enactment of the cosmic package; the Incarnation was its ardent unwrapping.

The movement between these two revelational and relational *loci* means that, post-initiatorily, cosmological evolution is the process of the natural revelation of God. Throughout, the Holy Spirit

38. Arthur Koestler coined the word *bisociation* to depict the creative process as the mixing of two ideas in the generation of novelty. See Koestler, *The Act of Creation*, 98.

39. Rahner, *Theological Investigations*, vol. 5, 171–72.

eternally indwells the process such that the fullness of supernatural revelation in Christ has flowed specially through time from the beginning, from whom it began ("He was in the beginning with God" John 1:2), to the end ("Then comes the end, when he delivers the kingdom to God the Father" 1 Cor 15:24). *That* cosmogenic flow, from beginning to end, persists in each now moment through God's spoken Word, which creates and redeems in the same utterance.

The following mysterious quote from Rahner, if taken as meaning God's intention in creation, makes more sense:

> The end is the absolute beginning. This beginning is not infinite emptiness or nothingness, but the fullness which alone explains the divided and that which begins, which alone can support a becoming and which alone can give to that which begins the real power of movement towards something more developed and at the same time more intimate.[40]

The beginning is not a move from nothingness to creation, but from God's infinite fullness to cosmic actuality through divine action. The beginning of the cosmos marked the gift of a creative movement from and by the pre-existent Other who is one with the Word, and who "was in the beginning with God" in the creative act. The power of that impetus sustains the cosmogenic movement that is cosmic-becoming, unfolding perpetually. That same eternally present One continuously provides the cosmos with the means to evolve into "something more developed and at the same time more intimate," through conjoining matter with spirit in human beings. Cosmogenic movement toward the intimacy that is the human embodied spirit made possible God's subsequent indwelling among us as one of us.

> But by the very fact that this movement of the development of the cosmos is thus carried along both from the outset and in all its phases by the urge towards ever greater fullness and intimacy and towards an ever closer and more conscious relationship to its ground, the message which says that there will be an absolutely

40. Rahner, *Theological Investigations*, vol. 5, 172.

> direct contact with this infinite cause, is already given in this movement—not indeed as something which must necessarily be recognized from this movement in all its phases, but at least as something which can certainly be more and more approximately envisaged as the absolute goal of this development.[41]

Indeed, who could have predicted that God would join with creation in the mystery of the hypostatic union? The Incarnation *is* "the absolute goal of this development."[42]

Biological evolution is the process by which physical reality possibly realized God's intention to instantiate human life. Cosmogenic evolution was and remains the generative dynamic, evidence of God's intention to create so that the Holy Spirit *could* indwell the universe, and that the Son *could* become incarnated in it as a person with both a divine and human nature.

The angels sang in joy at Jesus's birth because the entire universe was his manger. They have yet to cease.

41. Rahner, *Theological Investigations*, vol. 5, 172.

42. Rahner, *Theological Investigations*, vol. 5, 172.

On Beauty

In this essay, we discuss the intimate interiority of beings, considering their external beauty as a sign inviting us to the contemplation of being. We begin by looking at beauty in relation to ancient concepts that have traditionally supported the objective conviction of beauty's inextricability from the good and the true. We then observe what the Church Fathers recognized as our inadequacy in perceiving God's ineffable beauty as the source of all created being. Next, we explore how, after the Enlightenment, beauty was reduced to being a matter of subjective taste, albeit possessing a universal dimension emerging from the common categories of human perception—and how philosophy and theology have responded to this dilemma. Our consideration of these histories culminates in a question: What should be the quality of our dialogue with the beings of this place called Earth?

Early Thinking about Beauty

In Christian tradition, goodness, truth, and beauty are interchangeable aspects of being. Each thing has being; each is a being with these qualities. These "transcendental" attributes of being come to us from ancient Greek thought. Parmenides, and later Plato and Aristotle, did not treat all four transcendentals as equivalent to being or to one another. For Plato, ideal beauty was the only real beauty. He thought priority was to be given the good over the true. For Aristotle, from whom the term *transcendental* originates, unity applies to all being, but goodness and truth are qualities of rational creatures alone. He offered no notion of creation-out-of-nothing or even out of absolute being. The attributes of being, though derivative, were not directly contingent upon divine graciousness. For Plato, worldly beauty participated in being as a shadow of the ideal. Beauty and being are convertible concepts, that is, being is always and everywhere beautiful, and beauty is always and everywhere real. However, Plato's real world of ideal forms was not identical with the glory of the gods.

A much later Christian synthesis recognizes all four transcendentals as equivalent and inherent in each being as true, good, and beautiful in integral unity. All beings are representative of God's glory, each possessing a true beauty of its own. Christ is the nexus point in the cosmos sustaining all reality together in unity. Unlike Plato's version, the real in this synthesis is not centered elsewhere, and we do not experience mere projections of it. It is one with creation.

In creation, God imparts to everything a necessarily limited but intrinsic beauty. Unlike Aristotle, Scripture reveals each thing as good (Gen 1), and truth and light are one in the Word (John 1:1–9). In the Christian cosmos, God is *not* a vain participant like the Greek gods who manipulated human beings like game pieces. Christians recognized God as "with us." In Christ, God became both immanent and transcendent: intimately and eternally among us, and at the same time infinitely beyond the cosmos. It had to be this way for human freedom to be respected and to become capable of the grace of providential oversight.

Fathers of the Church

Influenced by Neo-Platonism, Gregory of Nyssa held that God is the archetype of beauty. Although earthly beauty is not merely a shadow of the real, full access to the archetype is not possible, neither in comparison to material beauty, nor in the expression of human language. Our only avail is to idealize the contingent by analogy. In *On the Making of Man*, Gregory interprets the image of

God as a divine self-portrait that only resembles divine beauty, but discloses God's power.

> It is true, indeed, that the Divine beauty is not adorned with any shape or endowment of form, by any beauty of color, but is contemplated as excellence in unspeakable bliss. As [w]hen painters transfer human forms to their pictures by the means of certain colors, laying on their copy the proper and corresponding tints, so that the beauty of the original may be accurately transferred to the likeness, so I would have you understand that our Maker also, painting the portrait to resemble His own beauty, by the addition of virtues, as it were with colors, shows in us His own sovereignty . . . [1]

In creating the finite cosmos, God rendered the divine self-image, a *necessarily finite* representation of his infinite beauty. God colored humanity with "purity, freedom from passion, blessedness, alienation from all evil, and all those attributes of the like kind which help to form in men the likeness of God: with such hues as these did the Maker of His own image mark our nature."[2] Humans participate in God's "hues"—the divine virtues—but only contingently, because of the Fall. Although the beauty of the cosmos is the image of God's glory, human language remains unable to express the excellence of the archetypal beauty. The quality of God's part in the dialogue cannot be complemented by our woefully unequal response. In our finitude, we miss a lot. In *On Virginity*, Gregory of Nyssa writes about this incapacity:

> We have not learned the peculiar language expressive of this beauty. An example of what we want to say does not exist in the world; a comparison for it would at least be very difficult to find. Who compares the Sun to a little spark? Or the vast Deep to a drop? And that tiny drop and that diminutive spark bear the same relation to the Deep and to the Sun, as any beautiful object of man's

1. Nyssa, *On the Making of Man*, in Schaff and Wace, *Nicene and Post-Nicene Fathers*, vol. 5, 391.

2. Nyssa, *On the Making of Man*, in Schaff and Wace, *Nicene and Post-Nicene Fathers*, vol. 5, 391.

> admiration does to that real beauty on the features of the First Good, of which we catch the glimpse beyond any other good.[3]

God's pre-eminence is beyond our cognitive capacity. We, the finite images of the divine Word, cannot be rendered as infinite beauty. And yet Gregory's equation of beauty with the "First Good" introduces a cross-concept that gives depth to the understanding of beauty without recourse to an example that "does not exist in the world." Having linked the good and the beautiful, he references truth, offering the example of David's vision and incapacity to do justice to their unity in being:

> Well does the great David seem to me to express the impossibility of doing this. He has been lifted by the power of the Spirit out of himself and sees in a blessed state of ecstasy the boundless and incomprehensible Beauty; he sees it as fully as a mortal can see who has quitted his fleshly envelopments and entered, by the mere power of thought, upon the contemplation of the spiritual and intellectual world, and in his longing to speak a word worthy of the spectacle he bursts forth with that cry, which all re-echo, "Every man a liar!" I take that to mean that any man who entrusts to language the task of presenting the ineffable Light is really and truly a liar; not because of any hatred on his part of the truth, but because of the feebleness of his instrument for expressing the thing thought of.[4]

The "ineffable Light" of truth is the only language that does justice to the beauty that is also goodness. We must settle for what we are able to discern of the ineffable.

Later, Pseudo-Dionysius the Areopagite also identifies God with divine beauty, writing that beauty pre-existed the cosmos as "superessential" beauty. Beauty is one of the names of God and part of the divine self-revelation, along with truth and goodness.

3. Nyssa, *On Virginity*, in Schaff and Wace, *Nicene and Post-Nicene Fathers*, vol. 5, 354.

4. Nyssa, *On Virginity*, in Schaff and Wace, *Nicene and Post-Nicene Fathers*, vol. 5, 354.

For Pseudo-Dionysius, beauty is the medium of recapitulation of God's intention for all things to attain oneness with God:

> From this Beautiful (comes) being to all existing things—that each is beautiful in its own proper order; and by reason of the Beautiful are the adaptations of all things, and friendships, and inter-communions, and by the Beautiful all things are made one, and the Beautiful is the origin of all things, as a creating Cause, both by moving the whole and holding it together by the love of its own peculiar Beauty; and end of all things, and beloved, as final Cause (for all things exist for the sake of the Beautiful) and exemplary (Cause), because all things are determined according to It. Wherefore, also, the Beautiful is identical with the Good, because all things aspire to the Beautiful and Good, on every account, and there is no existing thing which does not participate in the Beautiful and the Good. Yea, reason will dare to say even this, that even the non-existing participates in the Beautiful and Good.[5]

All beings without exception find their origin in Beauty. Hence our being is essentially beauty that is both true and good, but proper to being human. And in the beauty of all beings, in their proper order, "all things are made one" through the "creating Cause." Pseudo-Dionysius concludes that beauty is identical with the good and all things that participate in it, even those things that do not yet exist. We might say, from our perspective today, that when the unknown, yet to be discovered, finally comes to light in the ongoing unfolding of the cosmos, it will be intrinsically beautiful, the image of God's name. For the "non-existing" to participate in the beautiful and the good, he means those things yet to be created—truths potential in the mind of God. Thus, God establishes dialectic parameters for the future by endowing humanity with God-like transcendental qualities, making extant dialogue with us possible.

As we have seen, the Church Fathers' treatment of the transcendental attributes is centered on those attributes' interdefinability. The beauty, goodness, and truth of created things are autonomous attributes, united as one. They have God's glory

5. Dionysius the Areopagite, "On the Divine Names," 27–28.

as their source and point of departure, the fullness of which is beyond us.

Mediaeval Thought on Beauty

In the mediaeval period, scholars attempted to further characterize the intelligibility of the mystery of beauty. For Thomas Aquinas, beauty in the world is a transcendental property constituent of each autonomous created being. Our autonomy is limited and contingent upon God as efficient cause (the creator), ultimate cause (the purpose of existence or end toward which we move), and exemplar (the immeasurable standard of our existence). Each of us is autonomous from *but* derivative of God, who is infinitely Other.

Aquinas characterizes the essence of what it is to be human by drawing upon the divine essence as exemplar, thus distinguishing humans from God. Following Gregory of Nyssa and Pseudo-Dionysius, Aquinas sees human nature as distinctively human in the *image* of God, but not identical with God. Each has being: God supremely; we determinately. For Aquinas, the image of God is reflected in our intellect. Since beauty is a transcendental attribute of being, human beauty is to God as the imperfect is to the perfect. And as God cannot be seen, the glory of his infinite intellect is the intangible image of our unseen intellect. In Aquinas, beauty becomes unseen.

As sensate beings, we characterize beauty via visual qualities of light, clarity, proportion, and integrity. But visible light is not found in God. Divine radiance (*lux*) is unapproachable light. Aquinas sees *lux* as intelligible or spiritual clarity or radiance that is pleasing to the mind rather than to the senses. Thus, God has spiritual beauty of the highest kind. Beauty in an existent thing is its aesthetic splendor—for example, the visible color, order, and integrity of a flower. Yet it also has transcendental beauty—beauty that is *identical* with its being and can only be perceived by the mind and not the senses. *Only in this latter sense do we say that God is supremely beautiful.* There is no material aesthetic of divinity, because God is beyond sensibility. The paradox inherent in this apparent liability is that, like created truth and goodness, physical beauty is the only entry through which we can have access to God's ineffability. Beauty is a concept we use to inadequately represent ourselves as enacted attributes of divinity—an analogy for God's glory. Our access to the divine can only ever be through our inadequacies.

Immanuel Kant

In the eighteenth century, early modern scientists laid the intellectual groundwork for the scientific method. Kant anticipated what would become the ultimate object of scientific investigation by positing a measurable universe offering no indication of divine glory. Kant reasoned that if divine intention gave rise to the laws of the universe, there is no need for God's continued presence in it. He understood the kernel of religion to be morality; he saw no need for divine revelation, believing that religion should shed all doctrine and assent to "rational faith." For Kant, Christ is merely the standard of moral perfection, and glory is immanent rather than divine.

According to Kant, there are two things that fill the mind with admiration and awe: the sky above teeming with stars, and moral law within. The stars, planets, Milky Way, and northern lights had a noteworthy impact upon his philosophical system. In *Universal Natural History and Theory of the Heavens (1755)*, he writes:

> . . . the sight of a starry heaven on a clear night gives a kind of pleasure which only noble souls experience. In the universal stillness of nature and the tranquility of the mind, the immortal soul's hidden capacity to know speaks an unnamable language and provides inchoate ideas that are certainly felt but are incapable of being described.[6]

Kant denies that aesthetics is knowledge. One does not *know* judged objects to be beautiful; taste experiences merely pleasure or pain. "The judgment of taste is not a judgment of cognition, and

6. Kant, *Universal Natural History and Theory of the Heavens*, 421–22.

is consequently not logical but esthetical, by which we understand that whose determining ground can be *no other than subjective.*"[7] When we perceive a thing to be beautiful, we experience that it is so and presume that others do likewise. For Kant, there exists a common human competence in recognizing the beautiful. That is, even if beauty pleases me in my personal experience of it, it is still universally recognizable. Aesthetic sense is a common human attribute that is felt.

For Kant, beauty is a quality of sensible things that human taste recognizes by apprehension alone, without cogitative approval. This makes "knowledge" of beauty unlike theoretical knowledge, which is the province of the intellect. The experience of beauty can be communicated readily insofar as aesthetic experience is felt. Cultural norms of creativity therefore contribute to the expectation of a common aesthetic and moral sense. Notions of beauty are perpetuated through conditioning, familiarity, and expectation within the geographical and historical niches in which a given society develops. Kant believed that people generate beauty based on the standard of creativity that the dynamically evident cosmos provides as ground.

Kant affirms the unending creative process of the universe—that life advances constantly because of nature's infinite fertility. In his thought, experience of the divine is replaced by the innate sense of duty. The kingdom of God is thus achieved on earth through human moral action—recognition of and attendance to the good. In Kant's view, we need no day-to-day measure of grace, which theologically is the gift of glory. Whereas Newton understood the universe to need God the mechanic to tune the cosmological clockwork, Kant writes: "Creation is never accomplished. It has indeed once begun, but it will never cease."[8] In other words, the universe undergoes creation progressively and continuously, conforming conceptually with fluid cosmological unfolding.

After Kant, there was a cultural shift in speculation regarding the cosmos. He provided the philosophical impetus for challenging

7. Kant, *Critique of Judgment*, 51.

8. Kant, *Kant's Cosmogony*, 146.

the assumption of a static universe, anticipating instead the fluid and evolving universe embraced in the nineteenth century. The latter embrace would become the philosophical ground of the theory of evolution, which depicted the emergence of life as a continuum moving from seminal potency toward ever more complex and advanced forms. As if predicting this, Kant explains: "the developed world is bounded in the middle between the ruins of the nature that has been destroyed and the chaos of the nature that is still unformed."[9] A universe of change emerges ever anew from the destructive forces of nature in the very chaos it renders.

For Kant, such a universe should have the full potential to "become" continuously without direct divine direction, and to be recognizably beautiful via human common sense. Thus, unlike the mediaevals, for whom beauty was an attribute of each being, for Kant, aesthetic pleasure is subjective knowledge of the objective reality of natural beauty.

Theological Aesthetics and Science

The divorce of truth from beauty is philosophically entrenched in the scientific method. The Enlightenment gave birth to both movements—thus, if beauty is not knowledge, it cannot be a scientific datum either. The pursuit of tangible truth should be the only intent of science. Through the employment of its method, scientific knowledge grows apace in the continuous progress that characterizes contemporary human life. Science does not, cannot, record beauty *per se* if it is only a feeling. However, scientists do make use of the truths to which beauty attracts them. Beauty indicates truth, draws us toward it. This dynamic did not change in the divorce. Beauty not only pleases us; it conditions us. It persuades us that there is truth to be valued in our encounter with an object or idea or formula. Physics equations are deemed beautiful because of their symmetry and predictive abilities. A beautiful electron micrograph makes us enthused that data gleaned from it will be significant.

9. Kant, *Kant's Cosmogony*, 152.

It seems fitting that truth reciprocates the beauty of biological or mathematical form. Clearly, beauty and truth are linked in physical science, as is reason with our feelings—this despite recognition of beauty's failure to be an objectively measurable physical property (a failure accordant with beauty's transcendental character). The scientific object does not reveal the metaphysical reality of being, but only the sensible truth of things from which humanity can gain enduring benefit. Truth is thus the highest scientific goal, followed by the good that can be cleverly derived from it.[10]

Since beauty is not quantifiable or objectively determinable, it is not a scientific category for fact-gathering. Even when a protocol is used to gather qualitative data, beauty is not significant beyond the investigators' personal appreciation. An ecosystem under study can take one's breath away in the beauty of its variety and complexity. Data gleaned from it may be beautiful in its harmoniousness (consider the harmoniousness of ecosystems' food webs), evoking the unity of truth presumed to inhere in the biosphere, making it attractive and desirable but of no scientific avail. However, it is still valid to posit that the beauty-that-beings-are is being-in-unity.

In a scientistic mindset, the practice of seeking truth intended only for use has separated us from the beauty that attracts us to truth in the first place, thus fracturing that unity. This has been a regrettable outcome of the ideological scientization of culture. That beauty has been disarticulated from its unity with truth and goodness has become emblematic of the damage we have done to our home-world. Healing the divorce of beauty from truth should restore the way to wholeness, or at least begin the process. To do so requires a critique of the Enlightenment contention that aesthetics is purely sensate experience unrelated to truth.

Gadamer's Address to Science

The twentieth-century German philosopher Hans-Georg Gadamer's critical contribution to the question of beauty was his

10. It is elsewhere the province of moralists to dissect the meaning of good use.

insight into truth as disclosed in the work of art. In his philosophical meditations, he effectively reunites truth with beauty. In his lifetime, Gadamer feared that scientific truth would usurp all other legitimate forms of truth—that science would "consume" truth. He believed that the success of the natural sciences, and the peculiar form of truth derived from them, had led to a forgetfulness of the manifold other ways in which truth can be experienced. He contended that scientific truth is one experience of truth, but not the *only* one.

In everything we do as human beings, we are always already involved with truth not accessible to scientific verification—for example, the truth of art. Gadamer writes:

> The fact that through a work of art a truth is experienced that we cannot attain in any other way constitutes the philosophic importance of art, which asserts itself against all attempts to rationalize it away. Hence, together with the experience of philosophy, the experience of art is the most insistent admonition to scientific consciousness to acknowledge its own limits.[11]

For Gadamer, art is a manifestation of our creative actions to imitate nature. In his words, "Art is only 'possible' because the formative activity of nature leaves an open domain which can be filled by the productions of the human spirit."[12] Art, because it imitates nature, is not as "real" as the nature that it represents, but it does have its *own* reality, its being peculiar to its realization. Hence art also has all the attributes of being. The most immediately accessible attribute is beauty and in beauty, truth is disclosed.

The "truth" of the work of art is not scientific truth to be used for extraneous purposes. For the one who engages with it, art involves an investment that gains utility the object otherwise lacks on its own. Scientific research is ultimately for the intended utility of its truths in the practical world—particularly when industry and government dictate its purpose. Regardless of application, the truth sought in science is demonstrative, natural, and believed to

11. Gadamer, *Truth and Method*, xxii-xxiii.

12. Gadamer, *The Relevance of the Beautiful*, 13.

be "the case" in all instances. Art, however, is uniquely itself, intended only for itself. Says Gadamer: "The work has no real 'use' as such, but finds its characteristic fulfillment when our gaze dwells upon the appearance itself."[13] For Gadamer, *the work of art has its own reality or being; and in our gazing upon it, it reaches fulfillment in our experience of it.* The truth of the work of art is not conceptually or practically useful. Yet, in its disclosure and in our appreciation of it, it has truth to be valued.

Gadamer thus exposes the weakness of Kant's characterization of beauty. If beauty is only "felt," what can it be but inexpressible truth? Clearly, not all truth is expressible; some truths never will be. When a great work of art has a profound and shared effect upon all who see it, hear it, or read it, our experience cannot be communicated like a scientific fact. Gadamer writes that "when we take aesthetic satisfaction in something, we do not relate it to a meaning which could ultimately be communicated in conceptual terms."[14] There is interplay in our experience of beauty in a work of art that evokes a personal relationship. That art informs is not the point; the experience of art and its effect is.

The Anthropological Basis of Aesthetic Experience

Gadamer called the inability to conceptually communicate aesthetic satisfaction the anthropological basis of the aesthetic experience. The encounter with the beautiful is the basis of all engagement, including with natural beauty. The immediacy of our experience with the autonomy of the work of art is an unrecordable truth-experience. The inexpressible engagement with living being has a similar truth-experience in our encounter with it. Essayist Annie Dillard relates her aesthetic experience of an accidental encounter with beauty while hiking in the wild. She attempts to relate the effect it had upon her:

13. Gadamer, *The Relevance of the Beautiful*, 13.

14. Gadamer, *The Relevance of the Beautiful*, 13.

> The weasel was stunned into stillness as he was emerging from beneath an enormous shaggy wild-rose bush four feet away. I was stunned into stillness, twisted backward on the tree trunk. Our eyes locked, and someone threw away the key.
>
> Our look was as if two lovers, or deadly enemies, met unexpectedly on an overgrown path when each had been thinking of something else: a clearing blow to the gut. It was also a bright blow to the brain, or a sudden beating of brains, with all the charge and intimate grate of rubbed balloons. It emptied our lungs. It felled the forest, moved the fields, and drained the pond; the world dismantled and tumbled into that black hole of eyes.[15]

Dillard's encounter with the weasel was a mutual surprise. It was a shared moment beyond value, without use; a truth rooted in the moment. Her perception of the world was put on hold. It was a moment's experience of eternity in an encounter in shared beauty with another being. However, it did not last as such:

> He disappeared. This was only last week, and already I don't remember what shattered the enchantment. I think I blinked, I think I retrieved my brain from the weasel's brain, and tried to memorize what I was seeing, and the weasel felt the yank of separation, the careening splash-down into real life and the urgent current of instinct. He vanished under the wild rose. I waited motionless, my mind suddenly full of data and my spirit with pleadings, but he didn't return.[16]

The moment was lost as she "tried to memorize what [she] was seeing," as a datum to analyze. In a "yank of separation" from the encounter, objective distance was created and provided a cogitative space into which she slotted reportable truth. Friedrich Schelling would have said she made a "representation."[17] For neuroscience,

15. Dillard, "Living Like Weasels," 125.

16. Dillard, "Living Like Weasels," 125.

17. "When I represent an object, the object and the representation are one and the same. And it is only this inability to separate the object from the representation while one is representing it that convinces common understanding of

the sensory experience became processed at a higher level of the cerebral cortex. Maybe both are correct within their disciplinary limits, but naming cannot fully explain the shared experience in the encounter now lost.

> Please do not tell me about "approach-avoidance conflicts." I tell you I've been in that weasel's brain for sixty seconds, and he was in mine. Brains are private places, muttering through unique and secret tapes—but the weasel and I both plugged into another tape simultaneously, for a sweet and shocking time. Can I help it if it was a blank?[18]

Dillard eschews a scientific explanation because it cannot do justice to that "sixty seconds" of shared consciousness that was so meaningful that she wrote about it. Her account was so enchanting to me that I immediately knew what she meant, simultaneously regretting that I missed a unique moment that will never happen again even if the universe persisted for another 13.8 billion years.

In our personal engagement with beauty at the anthropological level, the truth apparent in the encounter cannot be communicated. In the attempt to communicate it, we create objective distance and characterize the real at arm's length, necessarily separating ourselves from the experience and the other. However, the unique personal experience of the individual with the being at hand is both personal and objective, because whatever we conclude in reflection afterwards, we still retain the unity of our original encounter with beauty. That truth can never be communicated in its fullness because it is ours alone. In every encounter with beauty, we are reassured of our personal uniqueness while united in it. Herein lies the transcendental quality of the encounter with beauty—beauty is every bit as much unitive as is truth and goodness. In fact, it is the gravity that holds them all together.

The truth of the scientific object, like that of the work of art, begins in the engagement with being. As scientists plumb the

---

the reality of external things, which in fact make themselves known to it only through representations." Schelling, "Ideas on a Philosophy of Nature," 170.

18. Dillard, "Living Like Weasels," 125.

depths beyond personal encounter, they immediately put the encounter aside and form an objectifying distance wherein abides the font of scientific fact. The two modes of engagement are inextricably linked. Only in a multidisciplinary embrace can we fully appreciate the beauty of the cosmos, and in that unity recognize the truth that we must preserve about our beautiful home.

Christ: The Form of Revelation

The beauty revealed in the Christ event brings new perspective to the Greek notion of the glory of the gods. In God becoming a man, earthly cooperation in divine glory becomes the fullest expression of the immanent beauty of creation. In the Incarnation, Hans Urs von Balthasar sees Jesus Christ as the form for created beauty. Christ is the ideal Form for human life, the unattainable ideal, and our only access to Incarnation. The mysterious admixture of human and divine is the agency by which God speaks directly to humanity. It is the "language" that allows our ingress into divine glory through the beautiful human life of Jesus. In the Christian synthesis, created being is *real* beauty. Hence, goodness and beauty are not just reflections of the ideal of divine being. Nor are they just duties or feelings peculiar to our nature. They are *real* qualities of autonomous created beings. We have access to the divine truth that Christ spoke, the divine goodness that he lived, and his unity with the Father through our common human experience of the beautiful. Christ's life represents the standard for what it is to live in God as one.

A purely Platonic notion of beauty cannot be used to interpret the Incarnation. Balthasar writes: "The image and expression of God . . . is the indivisible God-man: man in so far as God radiates from him; God, in so far as he appears in the man Jesus."[19] We cannot simply equate Jesus's human nature with the physical, and his divine nature with the spiritual, because human beings are both matter and spirit. There is a mysterious unity between human soul-embodiment and the divinity of the God-man. Balthasar writes:

19. Balthasar, *The Glory of the Lord*, 437.

> The glory of God is nowhere, not for a single instant, separated from the Lamb, nor is the light of the Trinity divorced from the light of Christ, the Incarnate Son, in whom alone the cosmos is recapitulated and elevated to the rank of the bridal City.[20]

The man Jesus is not a divine download or avatar, nor merely the instrumental expression of God's glory. He is God eternally self-expressed to humanity in and through a man. God thus has power to express spiritual realities corporeally, and we have power to perceive *corporeally* the spiritual reality of God.

Like Gadamer, Balthasar contrasts the evident with what is concealed, not in this case in the work of art, but in the Form of revelation in Jesus Christ. Balthasar sees the contrast between the disclosed and the concealed as a threefold tension. They are

> (1) The inner-world tension between the manifestness of the body and the hiddenness of the spirit; (2) the tension, rooted in creation, between the cosmos (as image and expression of a free God who in no way is compelled to create) and God himself; and (3) the tension, rooted in the order of grace and redemption, between the sinner who has turned away from God and the God who has revealed himself as redeemer in the concealment of the cross.[21]

The first tension is the mystery of body and spirit in the world. The second tension is the mystery of God's image adumbrated in creation. Although vast and complex, the cosmos does not even approach the infinite simplicity of its exemplar-source. The third tension is the mystery of human will, gifted with freedom but necessarily imperfect. Human will is only the *image* of the exemplar's, whose infinite freedom is unfathomable. In each of these three tensions, the ontological difference between God and humanity refracts evident reality. Through each, the hidden can attain disclosure, as lenses do sight.

The difference between the truth of science versus the truth of art is only a matter of emphasis. Balthasar contends that the truth

20. Balthasar, *The Glory of the Lord*, 438–39.

21. Balthasar, *The Glory of the Lord*, 441.

that we learn through science is about the Art of the Absolute, or theo-drama,[22] in which our cooperation is as witness. However, because science cannot address ultimate cause, and therefore does not regard God as artist, actor, or playwright, then our part in worldly drama can mistakenly lead us to be plagiarizers of the divine reality and dubious about the omnipotent will behind it.

Glory is the province of theology . . . or is it the other way around? Clearly, it is not characterizable. Science does not have the capacity or intention to recognize beauty as symbolic of glory. Good. Having already exploited truth by reducing it to mere utility, it is a relief that it cannot exploit beauty as well. The philosophical concepts and theological insights into the truth of the work of art enable us to see the created order as more than something we just use. God is the supreme dramatist and we are both characters in the play as well as the audience. In human drama, both actor and assembly are just human—self-expressing to like selves. We create beauty by peeking through the gap in the curtain at beauty's image.

In this sense, scientific innovation is a kind of art—creatively using pre-created matter newly refashioned for the good of humanity, constantly seeking what is hidden. However, in contrast to the traditional materials of the artist, who uses known things to create new works, scientists seek new knowledge of familiar things to provide the means of fashioning the utterly novel.

The Good and Beautiful Place: The Truth of Life and Reflexive Causality

A fundamental conundrum arises when we weigh applied scientific knowledge against the exigencies of human nature, specifically the desire for personal gain versus for the common good. Both ethical and political, this dilemma parallels the metaphysical reality of the dynamics of life, pertaining perceptually to the individual and conceptually to the whole. As a result, the pursuit of scientific

22. Balthasar sustained the metaphor of God as actor in the ongoing drama of creation throughout five volumes of his *Theo-Drama: Theological Dramatic Theory*.

knowledge for the benefit of all has a deep-seated and persistent downside. The danger inherent in scientific discovery is that the good, sought from its successes, when applied, is often not entirely wholesome. Invariably, the scientific object possesses inherent qualities, goods that are inherently advantageous to interested parties, and rightly so, but which might not be advantageous to others. Venomous snakes must be necessarily unaffected by their venom if they are to be effective in subduing their prey. The products of mining, oil, and nuclear industries generate immediately beneficial utility, but all generate counterweighing toxic by-products. The drug industry develops medications for specific conditions that always have side effects that are deleterious to unrelated physiological processes, sometimes deadly. Thus, in every case of scientific innovation, the complex qualities of each resulting object make its utility a mixed blessing beyond the truth derived from discovery. Maximizing utility against liability is crucial to attaining the greater good. Otherwise, everyone loses. Unfortunately, the greater good does not always motivate the marketing of discovery.

Regardless of the degree of professional altruism historically intended among discoverers, profit-motivated developers have not always shared charitable intentions. If one weighs an object's goodly features against deleterious qualities not yet known about it, and then mixes in human vice, one can easily find the good being overwhelmed by expedience—and particularly greed. This has ever been the formula for human progress, more prevalent historically than the modern myth of the scientist-hero who saves the day using test tubes and techno-gadgets. In the history of commerce, what was good for humanity was first what was best for profiteers, and all else was secondary. Greed is an urgency that has ever energized human culture.

But civilizations fall for a plexus of reasons, only one of them financial. Beyond humanity, each of the world's many living beings has a sacred right to a nurturing place in which to abide. None will benefit if the well-off (i.e., humans) also suffer the consequences of their recalcitrance by neglecting the wholesomeness of each lived-in interconnected place. This should be obvious. However reiterating, the self-evident is also self-defeating, or at best a waste of time. Even cats bury their scat. Why can't we?

In view of this very human conundrum, we turn to American theologian Alejandro Garcia-Rivera's insight into the theological importance of place, and ask ourselves: What have we done to our beautiful home and why don't we stop? When human life evolved, the dialogue between the biotic and abiotic earth disclosed a transformative truth. Not only did the universe become self-aware through humanity's agency, it also became reflexively self-determinate through human consciousness. The unconscious planetary changes that life had previously wrought on Earth suddenly became conscious when human beings willfully intended change for their exclusive good. The human contribution to life's dialogue began in earnest when the earliest farmers cleared the land to plant crops, and in the process began to domesticate the wild earth to their liking, often to the detriment of other living things. Village settlements developed into towns, cities, and civilizations, each intended for human benefit. Many good things came for us from those wondrous developments, including discovery, education, improved quality of life, and eventually the benefits of modern life.

Despite all good intentions, human-induced change was not always good for Earth as a whole. In fact, Earth has suffered significant harm ever since our species began to expand and prosper. And because we have always been of one substance with our home, our species has reaped the consequences, both the good and the ill. The true and beautiful unity of the biosphere, which existed before human life evolved as part of its integral unity, has lately suffered greatly from flawed human choices that have engendered some unbeautiful and inharmonious consequences. The shadow side of our imperfect intentions has predisposed our self-destructive tendencies to the path of least resistance. Intending good is no guarantee of actually doing it.

Since its appearance, life tended to evolve into other, sometimes more specialized, forms. The outcome of that global bio-action has "back-affected" the abiotic earth and thus altered the forces of geological evolution. Both abiotic and biotic matter have engaged in this co-causal dialogue. In effect, from the biotic perspective, life has self-regulated its evolution by altering the physical parameters of the abiotic matrix it inhabits. Earth could not have developed to its present geophysical form had life not evolved in this way. This reflexive causal mechanism is fundamental to the unfolding of both geological and biological evolution.

Earth is replete with examples of reverse bio-causality, whereby the more complex level of matter has a causal effect upon lower levels. For example, in a constant cycle, carbon is sequestered from the atmosphere and fixed into bio-matter, and vice versa. Forests accumulate it, enriching the soils in which they grow. Soil organisms perforate the soil, enabling nitrogen penetration to the depths, where bacteria metabolize it to enrich soil fertility. More dramatically, over the millennia, coral accumulate on the ocean bottom while geological forces raise thick coral strata above the surface, giving rise to coral mountains such as the Dolomites in northern Italy. There are many other examples of how life has altered the surface of the planet over the past three billion years. None has caused a greater change than oxygen production by cyanobacteria 2.45 billion years ago. After a billion years of its accumulation in the atmosphere, the process led to the evolution of multicellular life and eventually gave rise to humans, the most willful of all Earth-changers. The earth moves under our feet and always has.

As human population density increased following the appearance of the genus *Homo*, archeological evidence and historical documentation have shown that the geological environment has changed radically as a result of human presence. Until the establishment of organized social groups and agriculture, our ancestors were integrated into the global ecology with harmonious effect. However, once these cultural advances occurred, our obsession with "taming the wild" upset the original harmony. The Sahara Desert was once rich grassland where herders grazed livestock. Their actions helped accelerate grassland conversion into desert, which compounded incipient climate change in the region during the last Ice Age. Throughout the world, deforestation for the building of dwellings and ships led to soil erosion. For example, Ephesus, one of the greatest Mediterranean ship-building seaports of the ancient world, is now six miles inland.

All examples of reverse causal processes of the biotic with the abiotic have influenced the quality of human experience and radically affected the life of individuals and nations. Soil erosion, pollution, and exploitation of non-renewable natural resources continue unequivocally to degrade the environment that has sustained all life on Earth. Until recently, these were unintended self-destructive acts. Fortunately, natural geological forces, synchronically acting upon the biosphere and vice versa, can produce causal effects that can repair human degradation of the environment. Some damage is recoverable through the natural forces of "geo-genesis" continually reforming the earth. However, human intentionality has now contributed to extensive deleterious changes that were not extant prior to the evolution of our species. Throughout human history, willful technological change has variously backfired, often catastrophically. Thus, our unconscious self-destructive tendencies have also had reverse causal effects on the world beyond the conscious level. Our oneness with our environment is at odds with our very existence.

Even with the purest of intentions, we are also constrained by the endless fecundity of natural necessity. The world will never be entirely tamable despite our hubristic delusions at weather control. Indeed, working against nature could eventually result in self-annihilation. Rerouting a river may seem good *per se* but it can be catastrophic for other species. With the discovery of nuclear power, humanity unleashed a confusion of potencies that have been non-native to planetary geochemistry for nearly two billion years.[23] The harnessing of fissionable nuclear power has changed the world forever by making it possible for us to destroy all life,

23. Self-sustaining nuclear fission occurred in uranium deposits in sixteen separate areas within the Oklo and adjacent Okelobondo uranium mines in Gabon, Africa, for perhaps 100,000 years. See Meshik, "The Workings of an Ancient Nuclear Reactor," 82–91.

potentially instantly, or poison it with toxic nuclear waste. We know such things to be true through science and from our experience of the Second World War. Consequently, our detailed and ever-increasing knowledge of science has forever outpaced the culpable ignorance of our non-rational ancestors. We now *know* better. It's beyond merely the level of "should."

We may, from time to time, find ourselves engaged in a futile act of defiance against nature, shaking our fists at lightening. But despite our desire for unlimited freedom, being alive means willfully surrendering to the inevitability of natural forces. Iron will always rust; hurricanes will always destroy trailer parks; and insects will always be resistant to eradication—as they should be. None of these facts can we change and none were altered by our fall from grace with God. Perhaps this is the inevitable outcome of being successful toolmakers expelled from paradise. No tool, no intention, no free act of will can effect the impossible. Our choices are limited by necessities that no created freedom can overturn.

Humanity has the right to choose, but should not expect to attain to the infinite freedom of a *de novo* creator. This is where the concept of co-creator reaches its figurative limit. A human being cannot create *de novo*. We are by necessity only *ever* effector-agents of a creator who made us *de novo* for that purpose. We choose life because Life first chose *us*. All non-sapient beings cannot help but cooperate in the necessity of life's proliferation through their native intelligence. Only humans have the right to *be* wrong, and we will always be wrong when we choose self-deluded contrariety over freedom, God's gift of agency. *Human freedom resides only in the choice to cooperate as agents tasked as stewards to preserve the unity of created being, which necessarily includes ourselves . . .* because rejecting agency is not a choice at all, but self-annihilation. "The LORD God took the man and put him in the garden of Eden to till it and keep it" (Gen 2:15), not leave a mess for someone else to clean up.

The pristine wilderness that was once all over the globe is now but a memory. Human ignorance, which was once merely culpable, is now willfully shameful, like our politicians. If we are to preserve this beautiful earth in truth for the good of all living beings, the present trend toward affluent self-destruction must stop. There was a revolution in our understanding in the early twentieth century when we learned of the true vastness of space. Its near-infinite extent means that our theological understanding of the earth must also be modified. Garcia-Rivera writes:

> One of the greatest challenges in early Christian theology was how to speak of the creation, Incarnation, and ascension in terms of place. After all, how can one conceive of the creation if not as a place? How could one speak of Jesus born in Bethlehem and raised in Nazareth without a sense of place? How could one speak of Christ ascended into heaven, if heaven is not a place? Yet how can a God who transcends space and time and place be thought of as being in a place?[24]

The Garden was mythological place, the locus of creation, from which the progenitors of humanity were banished. Theologically, it was *the* primordial place where all life—human, nonhuman, and divine—once dwelled together in the glorious interconnected conviviality we now lack. From the ground looking up, the Garden is a biblical metaphor for earth. But, from heaven looking down, archetypically, it reflects the inner trinitarian life that is the universal Garden, and creation is its analogy. In Christ's humanity we share in trinitarian life, attaining to oneness with God through the Love of the Father that is the Holy Spirit. By abiding in the peace of Christ, we find our link back to paradisiacal Good, to which we aspire willfully and to which human nature hurtles necessarily. Our return to the forest-garden—the beginning that was lost and is still longed for as paradise not yet restored—depends on the integrity of our dialogue with nature. Life can only be intended by a being who is free and conscious, acting for itself on behalf of all living beings, especially those not possessed of choice. Else, a human agenda intended exclusively for humanity's benefit will achieve loss for all.

24. Garcia-Rivera, *The Garden of God*, 52.

Human beings, even though we intend our experience of life, remain subject to efficient happenstance, determined by natural forces always beyond our freedom to control. Nonhuman life subsists unwittingly as the effect of cosmological unfolding. Through will and intellect, we recognize eternal life and love as the idealized end of a happy human life in the revelation of God. Through revelation, divine being self-discloses as the answer-asking-the-question. Despite our powers of cognition, we cannot recreate ourselves in our own image by reverse causality, or prevent our personal physical demise, despite the successes of scientific progress. Finite life and living ultimately accrue from the eternal life of God.

If we posit a question, the answer must ultimately come from the Other and not the asker. The ultimate truth is revealed in the redemptive glory of the death that is the finite end of this life, and the beginning of life eternal.

The Last Breath

There is an admirable honesty about science and its method that strives, ever skeptically, toward truth. As a method, science keeps scientists honest by requiring them to keep their preconceptions to a minimum (never completely eliminating them, of course, because the pursuit of truth relies on the core assumption that truth is attainable). Reason, we presuppose, is the ground of all striving, of all learning, whether scientific or spiritual. But for every sense, for every ground of personal experience, there are many ways of learning and knowing. No one can exhaust the fullness of knowledge available to the senses, limited as they are, and even so, what is beyond sense is not necessarily beyond being or knowing.

The honesty of theology vis-à-vis its fundamental object—infinite being—inheres in its faithful acknowledgement of the revealed infinite One. The humility of theology resides in its drawing of no definitive conclusions beyond the initial embrace of the deposit of faith (κήρυγμα). *There can be no new truths of faith*, only new ways of conceptualizing them. God is indiscernible to the senses and cannot be proven empirically to exist or not exist. It is for this reason that science and the world of sense *must* be excluded from making any objective characterizations of divinity. However, scientists who embrace all modes of knowing can indeed believe in God while maintaining professional methodological skepticism—that is, by placing each method, science and theology, in its proper place—intent always on being efficacious in the truth that grounds both. Scientific methodology does not impede scientists from being children of the God who created the empirical object of science—the cosmos and all it contains.

Theological Finale

For a book on Christianity and life science to be complete, at least theologically, we must do justice to more than Christology, as vast and inexhaustible a topic though it is. The figure of Christ in his divine nature in relation to his human life was our way *into* the study of Christianity and life. In fact, it was the *only* way into study if we were to remain within the parameters of our theme. Christ is both the exemplar and impossible goal of all intentions of Christian believers—insofar as we are grounded in our freedom to choose and our willfulness to succeed.

Aspiring beyond, however, to *become* the archetype—the exemplar—would be *the* consummate act of hubris. That was the primordial sin of the serpent, who, as the highest created being, tried to usurp the one who created it. Adam tried to imitate its slithering ways. Try as we might to be Christ-like, we are not divine and never will be, and we *will* fail in all God-unabetted attempts to become more than we are. Christian life goes beyond the biologically measurable truths that we have amassed. The difficulty of defining the natural order; the elusiveness of characterizing its material complexity; the mysteriousness of its interpersonal reflexivity—all point to a wellspring of life and living that cannot be our own, originating in a source beyond us. Self-generation is a contradiction—the most obvious of delusions.

No matter how meticulously we characterize life in the natural order, we always find ourselves the observers of externally originating phenomena, generating from an unseen and unseeable realm of existence. Where from? The term *matrix* is a colloquial metaphor of a rectangular math array that does not do justice to what I mean here. If stretched to three dimensions, matrix suggests a scaffolding that underlies matter, implying a kind of energy or elusive stuff that holds it all together. What I mean is the underpinning of even *those* matrices—something that is extra-cosmic, beyond any imagining of this or any possible parallel universe alike or unlike ours—the source that made both the living and non-living possible in the first instance of becoming.

What holds civilization together besides sober restraint from nuclear hubris? What makes us hope for utopia while we poison ourselves in the fumes of our greatest accomplishments? To do justice to the relationship between Christianity and life, we must consider the complexity of the life of God, in whose image and likeness *we are*, and in whom we find our ultimate origin. As we have seen, no matter what we might say about absolute mystery, we can never say enough to do it justice. Any attempt we make at characterizing divine life can therefore only be, in comparison with eternity, a brief sketch, a superficial commentary.

Living God

Christians believe in one God or divine substance, who is a Trinity of three divine persons—the divine commune of love. In these meditations we have focused on the divinity of the man Jesus, because our humanity counterparts with his in the natural order. We cannot comprehend how God can also be a man, but we have an experiential way into understanding it. We relate to Jesus at the level of limited self-knowledge because we are human as he is. But Jesus, by his own words in Scripture, also relates divinely to God the Father. And the Holy Spirit, we have recognized, indwells the cosmos as the breath of life, bringing to life new corporeal ensoulments. According to trinitarian dogma, which developed over four centuries after Jesus's death, we believe that the relationship between the Father and Son *is* the love that is the Holy Spirit. Put simply, the divine love between the Father and Son is the divine person of the Holy Spirit, each person infinitely giving of the divine self to the others. God is not only the author of relationship; the inner divine life is the supreme expression of it. It is in this *relational* sense that we say that God is love. In his encyclical *Dominum et Vivificantum*, John Paul II writes:

> It can be said that in the Holy Spirit the intimate life of the Triune God becomes totally gift, an exchange of mutual love between the divine Persons and that through the Holy Spirit God exists in the mode of gift. It is the Holy Spirit who is the personal expression of this self-giving, of this being-love. He is Person-Love. He is Person-Gift.[1]

Thus, God is also gift. Three-way divine giving is both infinitely loving *and* infinite love. And as creation's font, gift-love overflows the trinitarian brim, enacting the cosmos as created gift, the image of gift-love. This is what Thomas Aquinas meant when he said God's being is infinitely actualized. God's act is equivalent to who God is. God is love who creates love. Love is qualitatively of two types: uncreated and created. Uncreated love is divine life. Created love is our life. In God's image, we *are* created love. Life is love-disclosed.

In contrast to God's actualized being, we exist humanly. Human love is not an act equivalent to its being. Our act of loving is a work in progress, ever moving toward what is unattainable alone. Yet we *do* love, in a created sort of way, more or less, sometimes but not always, quasi-exclusively, conditionally, and selfishly. We cannot give infinitely to one another, although we might want to. It is difficult for us to be fully giving for very long, because we weary easily. Giving infinitely out of finitude is a logical impossibility.

It is qualitative of divinity to be eternally giving, generating finitude from an infinite wellspring. If humans exhaustively self-give everything to others, as does God, leaving nothing for ourselves, then we would "be" no longer because our love is finite, unless sustained by divine grace. Not so for God. The Father gives infinitely of himself to the Son and the Holy Spirit, who reciprocate that infinite giving. The infinite giving of divine love can never be exhausted, only augmented as proffered gift. The human gift of love to others imitates God's gift of love to us. But we cannot know what "gift of love" means unless we come to the fullest realization of our gifted lives. And we cannot achieve the fullness of

1. John Paul II, *Dominum et Vivificantum*, sec. 10.

that realization until we give *of* our lives as completely as we can. We must give the very thing we seek to know, and hence come to know it more fully *in* the giving. In other words, we can only ever *extrapolate* what the intra-trinitarian life-love is from our deficient analogies of human interdependence.

Early on in the history of Christianity, great minds sought to understand triune life-love and formulated their understanding in the creeds. The Nicene Creed summarizes the essential doctrine about each person of the Trinity held by all Christian denominations. The third confession reads: "I believe in the Holy Spirit, the Lord and giver of Life." The Holy Spirit is the giver of created life. Gen 1:1–2 reads: "In the beginning God created the heavens and the earth . . . and the Spirit of God[2] was moving over the face of the waters." The Holy Spirit was at hand at the gifting of existence itself, ever enlivening the image and likeness of God in humanity. John-Paul writes:

> Thus, from the beginning, the Church also confesses the mystery of the Incarnation, this key-mystery of the faith, by making reference to the Holy Spirit. The Apostles' Creed says: "He was conceived by the power of the Holy Spirit and born of the Virgin Mary." Similarly, the Nicene-Constantinopolitan Creed professes: "By the power of the Holy Spirit he became incarnate from the Virgin Mary, and was made man.[3]

And later:

> . . . the mystery of the Incarnation was accomplished "by the power of the Holy Spirit." It was "brought about" by that Spirit—consubstantial with the Father and the Son—who, in the absolute mystery of the Triune God, is the Person-love, the uncreated gift, who is the eternal source of every gift that comes from God in the order of creation, the direct principle and, in a certain sense, the subject of God's self-communication in the order

2. The Hebrew reads *ruah Elohim*, meaning the breath of God, creative power.

3. John Paul II, *Dominum et Vivificantum*, sec. 49, para. 4.

> of grace. The mystery of the Incarnation constitutes the climax of this giving, this divine self-communication.[4]

The Holy Spirit is the source of created life and love through whom the Incarnation was "brought about." Not only is the triune God the giver of life, but the One who graciously saves the given.

When we hear the word *graciousness*, we picture one so giving that their whole demeanor and life is a gift to others. Graciousness is God's gift to created life out of self. When that self also loves you infinitely, the gift is beyond any we can imagine giving ourselves. Such unqualified munificence may elicit in us doubt arising out of personal experience of giving, we who give finitely no matter how generous we are. The munificence of the eternal giver of infinite love ever enlivens all life.

> In the mystery of the Incarnation, the work of the Spirit "who gives life" reaches its highest point. It is not possible to give life, which in its fullest form is divine, except by making it the life of a man, as Christ is in his humanity endowed with personhood by the Word in the hypostatic union. And at the same time, with the mystery of the Incarnation there opens in a new way the source of this divine life in the history of mankind: the Holy Spirit. The Word, "the first-born of all creation," becomes "the first-born of many brethren."[5]

The Holy Spirit gives and fosters human life toward its fulfillment by bringing about, through the Incarnation, the *certainty* of salvation for the human race. The Holy Spirit who makes us possible is the One breath of Love that makes us fruitful. Our peculiar gifts distinguish us in our uniqueness from others. The shared gift of life finds expression in love that unfurls in the ongoing harmonization of our particularities. Love is the core mystery of being human. Though each of us is uniquely gifted, love fosters *because* of our differences.

4. John Paul II, Dominum et Vivificantum, sec. 50, para. 1.
5. John Paul II, Dominum et Vivificantum, sec. 52, para. 1.

Our personal gifts are wonders we manifest in the world through our corporeality, for our fulfillment and our inextricable link with others. The origin of all gifts is in the charismatic grace of the Holy Spirit, who gives them creatively and empowers their manifestation in the world. The Lord and Giver of Life continually gives to those who, in freedom, are open to receiving. Faith, the ultimate gift, enables human freedom to be expressed.

> And faith, in its deepest essence, is the openness of the human heart to this gift: to God's self-communication in the Holy Spirit. Saint Paul writes: "The Lord is the Spirit, and where the Spirit of the Lord is, there is freedom." When the Triune God opens himself to man in the Holy Spirit, this opening of God reveals and also gives to the human creature the fullness of its freedom.[6]

The fullness of created freedom is thus synonymous with human life. The creator spirit enabled the freedom-potential in our human nature—expressible in our self-reflectivity, empowered by the grace peculiar to its manifestation in our lives—and imparting a freeing effect on the world. The Holy Spirit enlivened the life and work of Jesus on earth. In fact, the Holy Spirit has always indwelled the universe, enlivening and preserving it in being. The prodigality of both the non-living and living cosmos finds its ultimate origin in the love that *is* the Holy Spirit.

Divine life is manifested in the physical universe through vague image and sketched likeness. Life and universe are the objects of science; both find their source in God. Science can neither characterize nor theorize about the life of the triune God; nor can engineers mimic it—nor *should* they, except in faithful communion. We avail ourselves of triune grace that enlivens all our deeds of goodness, our honoring of truth, and our finite attempts to steward our beautiful world. We unite our efforts in faith and freedom, and in the knowledge that we attain by analogy of triune life-love.

6. John Paul II, Dominum et Vivificantum, sec. 51, para. 2.

Bibliography

Aquinas, Saint Thomas. *Summa Theologica*. Translated by Alfred J. Freddoso. Self-published, 2018. https://www3.nd.edu/~afreddos/summa-translation/TOC.htm.

Augustine, Saint. *City of God*. Translated by Marcus Dods. Vol. 2 of *Nicene and Post-Nicene Fathers: First Series*, edited by Philip Schaff. Buffalo, NY: Christian Literature, 1887.

———. *Confessions*. Translated by R.S. Pine-Coffin. Harmondsworth, Middlesex: Penguin, 1961.

———. *On Genesis*. Translated by Edmund Hill, OP. Edited by John E. Rotelle, OSA. Vol. I/13 of *The Works of Saint Augustine: A Translation for the 21st Century*. New York: New City, 2002.

Balthasar, Hans Urs von. *The Christian and Anxiety*. Translated by Dennis D. Martin and Michael J. Miller. San Francisco: Ignatius, 2000.

———. "On the Concept of the Person." *Communio* 13:1 (1986) 18–26.

———. *Cosmic Liturgy: The Universe According to Maximus the Confessor*. Translated by Brian E. Daley, SJ. San Franciso: Ignatius, 2003.

———. *The Moment of Christian Witness*. Translated by Richard Beckley. San Francisco: Ignatius, 1994.

———. "A Résumé of My Thought." Translated by Kelly Hamilton. *Communio* 15:4 (1988) 468–73.

———. *Seeing the Form*. Vol. 1 of *The Glory of the Lord: A Theological Aesthetics*, translated by Erasmo Leiva-Merikakis, edited by Joseph Fessio, SJ and John Riches. San Francisco: Ignatius, 1982.

———. *Truth of the World*. Vol. 1 of *Theo-logic: Theological Logical Theory*, translated by Adrian J. Walker. San Francisco: Ignatius, 2000.

———. *The Word Made Flesh*. Vol. 1 of *Explorations in Theology*, translated by A.V. Littledale and Alexander Dru. San Francisco: Ignatius, 1989.

Barr, Stephen M. "The Evolution of Design." *First Things* 156 (October 2005) 9–12.

Benz, Ernst. *Evolution and Christian Hope: Man's Concept of the Future From the Early Fathers to Teilhard de Chardin*. Garden City: Anchor, 1968.

Brooks, Haxton. trans. *Fragments: The Collected Wisdom of Heraclitus*. New York: Viking, 2001.

Corazzon, Raul. "Selected Bibliography on Heidegger's Interpretation of *Aletheia* as Unconcealment." *Theory and History of Ontology*. Self-published, *ontology.co*, 2010. https://www.ontology.mobi/website-pdf/ontology.pdf.

Dessain, Charles S. and Thomas Gornall, eds. *A Grammar of Assent, January 1868 to December 1869*. Vol. 24 of *The Letters and Diaries of John Henry Newman*. Oxford: Clarendon, 1973.

Dillard, Annie. *The Annie Dillard Reader*. New York: HarperPerennial, 1994.

Dionysius the Areopagite. *Works*. Translated by John Parker. London: James Parker, 1897.

Gadamer, Hans-Georg. *The Relevance of the Beautiful and Other Essays*. Translated by N. Walker. Edited by Robert Bernasconi. Cambridge: Cambridge University Press, 1986.

———. *Truth and Method*. rev. ed. Translated by Joel Weinsheimer and Donald G. Marshall. New York: Continuum, 1999.

Garcia-Rivera, Alejandro. *The Garden of God: A Theological Cosmology*. Minneapolis: Fortress, 2009.

Gregory of Nyssa, Saint. *Gregory of Nyssa: Dogmatic Treatises*. Vol. 5 of *Nicene and Post-Nicene Fathers, Second Series*, edited by Philip Schaff and Henry Wace, translated by H.A. Wilson. Buffalo, NY: Christian Literature, 1893.

Irenaeus, Saint. *The Apostolic Fathers with Justin Martyr and Irenaeus*. Vol. 1 of *Ante-Nicene Fathers*, edited by Alexander Roberts, Sir James Donaldson, and A. Cleveland Coxe. Buffalo, NY: Christian Literature, 1885.

Jerome, Saint. *Theodoret, Jerome, Gennadius, Rufinus: Historical Writings*. Vol. 3 of *Nicene and Post-Nicene Fathers, Second Series*, edited by Philip Schaff and Henry Wace. Buffalo, NY: Christian Literature, 1892.

Jewish Virtual Library. "Issues in Jewish Ethics: Judaism's Rejection of Original Sin." https://www.jewishvirtuallibrary.org/judaism-s-rejection-of-original-sin.

John Paul II (pope), Vatican website. May 18, 1986. http://www.vatican.va/holy *Dominum et Vivificantum*. Encyclical letter. http://www.vatican.va/content/john-paul-ii/en/encyclicals/documents/hf_jp-ii_enc_18051986_dominum-et-vivificantem.html.

Kant, Immanuel. *Kant's Cosmogony. As in his essay on the retardation of the rotation of the earth and his natural history and theory of the heavens*. Edited and translated by W. Hastie, DDiv. Glasgow: James McLehose & Sons, 1900.

———. *Critique of Judgment*. Translated by J.H. Bernard. New York: Hafner, 1951.

———. *Universal Natural History and Theory of the Heavens*. Translated by Ian Johnston. Arlington, Virginia: Richer, 2009.

Kierkegaard, Søren. *Concept of Anxiety: A Simple Psychologically Orienting Deliberation on the Dogmatic Issue of Hereditary Sin*. Vol. 8 of *Writings*, edited and translated by Reidar Thomte in collaboration with Albert B. Anderson. Princeton: Princeton University Press, 1980.

Kilby, Karen. "Balthasar and Karl Rahner." *The Cambridge Companion to Hans Urs von Balthasar*. Edited by Edward T. Oakes, SJ and David Moss. Cambridge: Cambridge University Press, 2004, 256–68.

Koestler, Arthur. *The Act of Creation*. London: Hutchinson, 1964.

Liu, Joseph. "Scientists and Belief." *Pew Research Center*. https://www.pewforum.org/2009/11/05/scientists-and-belief.

Lococo, Donald J. "Freedom and Intimacy in von Balthasar's Theologic-I." *Analecta Hermeneutica*. 1 (2009) 114–35. https://journals.library.mun.ca/ojs/index.php/analecta/article/view/10.

Maimonides, Moses. *The Guide for the Perplexed: Unabridged Edition*. Translated by Michael Friedlander. New York: Cosimo, 2007.

Meshik, Alex P. "The Workings of an Ancient Nuclear Reactor," *Scientific American* 293(5) 82–91.

Pius XII (pope). *Humani Generis*. Encyclical letter. Vatican website. August 12, 1950. http://www.vatican.va/content/pius-xii/en/encyclicals/documents/hf_p-xii_enc_12081950_humani-generis.html.

Rahner, "Christology Within an Evolutionary View of the World." In *Theological Investigations*, vol. 5. Translated by Karl-H. Kruger. Baltimore: Helicon, 1966.

———. *Foundations of Christian Faith: An Introduction to the Idea of Christianity*.

Translated by William V. Dych. New York: Crossroad, 1982.

———. *Hominisation: The Evolutionary Origin of Man as a Theological Problem*. Translated by W.T. O'Hara. Freiburg: Herder, 1965

———. "Natural Science and Reasonable Faith." In *Theological Investigations*, vol. 21. Translated by Hugh M. Riley. New York: Crossroad, 1988.

Rice University. "First worldwide survey of religion and science: No, not all scientists are atheists." *Phys.Org*. https://phys.org/news/2015-12-worldwide-survey-religion-science-scientists.html.

Rolbiecki, J. J. "Ratio." *Dictionary of Philosophy*. http://www.ditext.com/runes/r.html.Rue, Loyal D. *By the Grace of Guile: The Role of Deception in Natural History and Human Affairs*. Oxford: Oxford University Press, 1994.

Schelling, Friedrich Wilhelm Joseph. "Ideas on a Philosophy of Nature as an Introduction to the Study of This Science." 2nd ed., 1803. In *Philosophy of German Idealism*, edited by Ernst Behler. New York: Continuum, 1987.

Smith, Reginald. "Complexity in Animal Communication: Estimating the Size of N-Gram Structures." Cornell University. http://arxiv.org/abs/1308.3616.

Thomson, Keith Stewart. "Marginalia: Huxley, Wilberforce and the Oxford Museum." *American Scientist* 88:3 (2000) 210–13.

University of Texas at Austin. "Evolution imposes 'speed limit' on recovery after mass extinctions." *ScienceDaily*. www.sciencedaily.com/releases/2019/04/190408114252.htm.

Wasmann, Erich. "Catholics and Evolution." *The Catholic Encyclopedia*, vol. 5. New York: Robert Appleton, 1909. http://www.newadvent.org/cathen/05654a.htm

Index

Abiotic, 49, 54, 79, 80–1
Act, 7–8, 16, 21, 26–28, 43, 48–49, 52, 54, 56–57, 57n38, 58, 82, 88, 90
Action, 7–8, 44–45, 54, 58, 68, 71, 79–80
Activity, 2, 4, 44, 50, 71
Actor, 77, 77n22
Adam, 28–34, 47n13, 88
Adam and Eve, 31–33
Adult, 28
Aesthetic experience, 68, 72
Aesthetics, 67, 69–70
Agency, 24n36, 50, 57, 75, 79, 82
Agent, 26, 29n45, 54, 82
Aletheia, 14, 14n3, 20
Animal(s), 17n13, 19, 19n22, 20, 22, 50, 55
Animate, 13, 14
Anxiety, 8, 28, 29–35
Aquinas, Thomas, 11, 51, 66, 90
Archetype, 13, 30, 62, 88
Aristotle, ix, 51, 61–62
Art, 71–77
Augustine, 30, 30n47–8, 40, 40n5, 41n6, 51, 51n22

Balthasar, Hans Urs von, xi, 4, 4n2–3, 5–6, 6n5, 7–8, 8n7–8, 9, 9n9, 14, 14n4–7, 15, 15n8–9, 16, 16n10–1, 17, 17n12–15, 18, 18n16–7, 18n19, 19, 19n20–1, 20n23–4, 21n25, 21n27, 22n28–31, 23, 23n32–3, 24, 24n34, 25, 25n37–9, 26n40–1, 27, 27n42, 29, 29n44, 31n49–50, 32, 32n51, 32n–53, 33, 33n54, 24, 24,55–7, 35n58–9, 35n61, 50, 75, 75n19, 76, 76n20–1, 77, 77n22
Beautiful, 62–71, 71n12, 72, 72n13–14, 75, 77, 79, 83, 93
Beauty, x, 5–8, 18, 61–84
Becoming, 17, 25, 48–49, 54–58, 75, 89
Being, ix, xi, 1–3, 6–10, 13–35, 39–40, 42, 45, 51–8, 61–75, 78–79, 82–84, 87–88, 90, 92–93
Beings, 10, 13–23, 27, 30n48, 42, 46–47, 49, 53–54, 58, 61–62, 65–66, 70–71, 75, 78–79, 82–84
Biosphere, 26, 48, 70, 79, 81
Biotic, 52, 54–55, 79–81
Birth, 10, 38n2, 52, 59, 69
Bisociation, 57

Cause, 3, 29, 34, 42, 48, 51, 59, 65–66, 77
Certainty, 28–29, 31–33, 35, 92

Index

Childhood, 33
Childlike, 31
Children, 28, 44, 86
Christ, x, xi, 7–10, 19, 35, 45, 58, 62, 67, 75–76, 83, 88, 92
Christian, ix, x, xi, 3–5, 8–9, 10n10, 15, 28–29, 29n44, 31n49–50, 32n51, 32n53, 33n54, 34n55–57, 35n58–9, 35n61, 37n1, 38, 38n2, 42, 51, 53, 61–62, 75, 83, 88, 91
Christianity, ix, x, xii, xv, 1, 4, 28, 88–89, 91
Christology, xi, 9, 54–55, 88
Civilization, 78–79, 89
Cognition, 15, 25, 27, 55, 67, 84
Communicate, 19n22, 68, 72, 74
Communication, 9, 19n22, 21–22, 25–26, 91–93
Conceal, 14–15, 27, 75–76
Consciousness, 8, 15–21, 23–27, 49–50, 54, 69, 71, 74, 79
Contingence , 6, 28
Contingent, 4, 31, 47n13, 53, 56–57, 62, 66
Corporeal, 2, 4, 76, 89, 93
Cosmogenesis, 38, 54, 56
Cosmos, xii, 2, 9, 38, 40, 46, 48, 53–58, 62–65, 68, 75–76, 88–90, 93
Created being, 7, 13, 23, 29, 46–49, 55, 57, 61, 66, 75, 82, 88
Creation, 5–7, 10, 13, 15, 28, 30–32, 37–52, 56–59, 62, 68, 75–77, 83, 90–92
Creator, 8, 16, 28, 31–32, 44, 47, 55, 66, 82, 93
Culture, xv, 1–2, 5–6, 10, 70, 78

Darwin, x, 37–39
Death, 7, 10, 30n46, 33, 50, 84, 89
Deception, 24
Dialogue, ix, xi, 1, 3, 5, 22, 37, 40, 42, 45, 61, 63, 65, 79–80, 83
Dillard, Annie, 72–74
Disclosed truth, 21, 26
Discretion, 16, 25
Divine, x, 2, 4, 7–10, 13, 15, 28–35, 37n1, 40–47, 53–59, 62–69, 75–77, 83–84, 88–93
Divine Action, 7, 58

Elijah, 35
Embodied spirit, 10, 33, 53–58
Emotions, 26
Enlightenment, 61, 69–70
Ephesus, 81
Exemplar, 10, 65–66, 76, 88
Eve, 30–31
Evil, 31, 33, 46, 63
Evolution, xii, 9, 24, 37–45, 48–49, 52, 54–55, 57, 59, 69, 80–81
Evolutionism, 52

Faith, 1, 3–6, 9–10, 30–31, 33–35, 38, 41–42, 45, 53, 67, 87, 91, 93
Faithful, 28, 32–33, 41, 87, 93
Fall, The, 29n45, 55n34, 63
Fathers of the Church, 6, 52, 62
Fertility, 68, 80
Finite, xi, 6, 13, 18, 20, 28–29, 31, 47–50, 63–64, 84, 90, 93
Foreknowledge , 4
Form, xi, xii, xvi, 2, 16, 21, 33, 39, 46, 50, 56, 63, 70–71, 75–76, 80, 92
Forms, 16, 26, 38–39, 41, 62–63, 69, 71, 79
Freedom, ix, xii, 3–8, 13, 13n1, 14–28, 30–31, 33, 47n13, 50, 54, 62–63, 76, 82, 84, 88, 93

Gadamer, 70–72, 76
Garcia-Rivera, 79, 83, 83n24
Garden, 28, 30, 55, 82–83
Gift, xvi, 7, 9, 16, 20, 25–26, 54–55, 58, 68, 74, 82, 90–93

Index

Glory, 7–8, 10, 62–63, 65–68, 75–77, 84
God, ix, xii, 2–10, 13, 15, 19, 23, 27–35, 37–59, 62–66, 68, 75–77, 82–84, 87–93
- Father, 8, 10, 34, 58, 75, 83, 89–91
- Holy Spirit, 4, 9, 35, 54, 56–57, 58, 83, 89–93
- Self-revelation, 34, 38, 57, 64
- Son, 8–10, 34, 42, 54, 59, 76, 89–91

God-man, 19, 34, 75
Good, ix, 24, 26, 32–33, 46, 61–62, 64–65, 68, 70, 77–79, 81, 83
Goodness, 7, 24, 28, 61–62, 64–65, 67, 70, 74–53, 93
Grace, 4, 8–9, 31, 48–49, 55–56, 62, 68, 76, 82, 90–93
Graciousness, 62, 92
Gregory of Nyssa, x, 7, 51, 51, 51n20, 63, 63n1–2, 64n3–4, 66

Heaven, 40, 53, 67, 83
Heidegger, 14
Heraclitus, 18
Hominization, 48, 50–52, 55–56
Hope, 5, 33, 89
Hubris, 28, 81, 88–89
Human, x–xi, 2–7, 9–10, 13, 15, 17–35, 38, 40–41, 44–47, 49–59, 61–63, 65–69, 71, 75–84, 88–93
- body, 38, 45–46, 50–55, 76
- freedom, xii, 3–4, 7, 13, 21–23, 27, 30, 47n13, 62, 82, 93
- life, 3, 10, 24, 30, 33–34, 40, 50–51, 54, 59, 69, 75, 79, 84, 88, 92–93
- nature, xi, 10, 28, 33, 54, 59, 66, 75, 77, 83, 93
- soul, 26, 38, 46, 50–55, 57, 75

Humanity, xi, 2, 6–10, 13, 17, 24, 28, 32, 34, 46, 53, 55, 63, 65, 70, 75–79, 81–83, 89, 91–92
Hypostatic union, 10, 59, 92

Image, 7, 10, 13, 15, 19–20, 30–31, 43, 57, 62–66, 75–77, 84, 89–91, 93
Image and likeness, 7, 30, 43, 57, 89, 91
Inanimate, 13–14
Incarnation, 8, 34, 45, 54–55, 57, 59, 75, 83, 91–92
Ineffable, 3–4, 57, 61
- light, 64

Infinite, 6–7, 13–14, 16, 18, 27, 30–31, 44, 4–48, 50, 57–59, 63–64, 66, 68, 76, 82–83, 87, 90, 92
Infinite being, xi, 7, 87
Infinitely, 13, 18, 31, 33, 45–46, 62, 66, 89–90, 92
Infinity, 3, 8, 13, 15, 26
Inflation, 49n17, 51, 57
Intellect, 6–7, 17, 19, 32, 41, 41n6, 64, 66–68, 84
Intention, xii, 26, 40, 43–45, 54, 58–59, 65, 67, 77–79, 81–82, 88
Intentionality, 40, 81
Interdependence, 22, 91
Interdependent, 23
Interiority, 14–20, 22–27, 49, 56, 61
Interpersonal, 88
Intersubjectivity, 18
Intimacy, 18–19, 22, 26–28, 34–35, 50, 58
Intuition , 26
Invisible, 27, 35
Irenaeus, 30, 30n46, 30n48

Jerome, 51
Jesus, 4, 6–7, 10, 19, 34, 45, 57, 59, 75–76, 83, 89, 93

Index

John-Paul II, 89–93

Kant, 67, 67n6, 68, 68n7–8, 69, 69n9, 72
Kierkegaard, 32, 32n52
Knowledge, x, xi, 8, 13–16, 18, 25–27, 31–32, 44, 51, 67–69, 77–78, 82, 87, 89, 93

Lamarck, 39
Language, xvi, 19, 21–23, 44, 62–64, 67, 75
Light, 6, 9, 19, 23, 40, 55, 61–62, 64–67, 69–70, 76, 82,
Living, xv, 15, 18, 21, 23, 26–28, 34–35, 39, 48, 52–54, 57, 72–74, 78–79, 83–84, 88–89, 93
Logos, 41–42, 45,
logos, 40–42, 45
Love, 7, 20, 30–31, 34, 43, 45, 65, 73, 83–84, 89–93
  created, 90
  divine, 89–90
  human, 90
  infinite, 7, 90, 92
  uncreated, 90
Lux, 66

Materialism, 2–5
Matter, xii, 2, 30n48, 37n1, 46, 49, 53–55, 57–58, 61, 75–77, 80, 88–89, 92
Maximus the Confessor, x, 4, 4n2–3, 7
Medical research, 22
Metaphysics, x, xii, 4, 41
Myth, 78
Mythological, 30–31, 50, 83

Natural selection, xii, 39, 43
Nature, ix, xi, 2, 7, 10, 14, 21–22, 25, 27–29, 33–35, 45, 48–49, 53–54, 56, 59, 63, 66–69, 71, 74–75, 77, 81–83, 88, 93
Neo-Platonism, 51, 62
Newman, John Henry, 37n1
Nicene Creed, 91
Nothing, 28, 32–33, 43, 58, 62, 90
Nothingness, 32, 58,
Nonhuman, 16–17, 19, 21, 27, 53, 81
Non-rational, 82

Object, 2, 17, 19, 25, 27, 45, 63, 67, 69–71, 73n17, 74, 78, 87–88
Objective, 22, 24, 27, 61, 69–70, 74–74, 87
Ontological difference, 29, 76
Original Sin, 28–30, 33

Pantheistic, 47
Parmenides, 61
Pius xii, 38, 52, 52n25
Place, 31, 33, 43n9, 48, 57, 61, 70, 77–79, 83, 87
Planet(s), xii, 54n32, 67, 79–81
Plants, 16–17, 21
Plato, ix, 51, 53, 61–62, 60
Platonic, 53, 75
Process thought, 3–5, 56n35,
Przywara, 7
Pseudo-Dionysius, 64–65, 65n5, 66–67

Rahner, Karl, xi, 5–6, 8–9, 9n10, 10, 10n10, 37–38, 45, 45n10, 46, 46n11–12, 47–8, 48n14, 49, 49n15–16, 50, 50n19, 52n27, 53n28–30, 55, 55n33, 56, 56n35–7, 57, 57n39, 58, 58n40, 59n41–2
Ratio, 41
Rational, x, 9, 21n27, 37, 41, 50, 55, 62, 67, 69
Redeemer, 33–34, 76
Redemption, 33–34, 76

Index

Resurrection, 7, 9–10
Reveal, 14, 25, 70
Revealed, x, 7, 15, 24, 34, 37n1, 54, 75–76, 84, 87
Revelation, ix, x, 8–9, 14, 16, 25, 31, 34, 38, 42, 47–48, 57–58, 64, 67, 75–76, 84
Reverse causality, 84
Random chance, 43

Salvation, 92
Schelling, 73, 74n17
Scientific object, 2, 45, 70, 74, 78
Scientific research, 14, 43, 71
Scientism, x, xi, 3, 68
Secondary causality, 49–50
Self-aware, 19–20, 50, 54–55, 79
Self-consciousness, 15–17, 20–24, 27
Self-destruction, 83
Self-possession, 23, 27, 57
Self-transcendence, 49, 55–56
Sense organs, 19, 26
Senses, 32, 34, 48, 51, 66, 87
Sensible, 2, 68, 70
Sensorium, 17, 20, 26
Sextus Empiricus, 42
Sin, 10, 28–30, 32–34, 47, 88
Sinfulness , 30
Solitude, 20, 23
Soul, 26, 38, 46, 50–57, 75
Spirit, 1–5, 9–10, 16, 23, 25–27, 33, 35, 45–46, 50, 53–59, 64, 66, 71, 73, 75–76, 83, 87, 89–91
Spiritual, 16, 26, 45, 53–54, 57, 64, 66, 75–76, 87
Subject, ix, 17–20, 25–27, 40, 47, 84, 91
Subjective, 19–20, 22, 24–25, 27, 35, 61, 68, 69
Sub-rational, 20, 22, 24
Supernatural, 48, 55–57

Theological aesthetics, 69–70
Theology, x–xii, 3, 5–9, 13, 27, 37–38, 40–42, 46, 48–49, 54, 61, 77, 83, 87
Transcendence, ix, 29, 32, 47n13, 49, 53, 55–57
Transcendental, 7, 24, 49, 61, 65–66, 70, 74
Transcendentals, 7, 61–62
Trinity, 76, 89, 91
Triune, 9, 87–91
Truth, ix–xi, 2, 5, 7–8, 13–18, 21, 23–26, 37, 41–42, 45, 61–62, 64–65, 67, 69–79, 83–84, 87–88, 93

Ultimate origin, 1–3, 8, 13, 40–41, 47, 52, 56, 64, 74, 82, 89, 93
Unity, x–xi, 10, 23, 35, 41, 45–46, 50–54, 61–62, 64, 70, 74–75, 79, 82
Universe, 2–4, 38, 41, 46–47, 49, 52–55, 56, 59, 67–69, 74, 79, 89, 93
Use, xii, 9, 25, 43, 67, 69–70, 72–74, 77
Utility, 71, 77–78

Visible, 66

Wallace, Alfred, 38
Weasel, 73–74
Wisdom, 6, 20, 41–42
Work of art, 71–72, 74, 76–77

www.ingramcontent.com/pod-product-compliance
Lightning Source LLC
Chambersburg PA
CBHW071051090426
42737CB00013B/2325
* 9 7 8 1 7 2 5 2 9 7 2 7 2 *